ANYONE CAN SING

ANYONE CAN SING

How to Become the Singer You Always Wanted to Be

Joan Wall and Ricky Weatherspoon

Graphics by: The Visual Group
Ernest Ludwick & Gary Hunt

* * *

DOUBLEDAY & COMPANY, INC., GARDEN CITY, NEW YORK 1978

Lyrics from "Waltzing Matilda"/music by Marie Cowan and words by A. B. (Banjo) Paterson. Copyright 1938 by Allans Music Australia Pty Ltd, Melbourne. Copyright renewed 1966 by Carl Fischer Inc., New York. Reproduced by permission of the copyright owners.

Excerpts from *Music In Therapy* by E. Thayer Gaston. © Copyright Macmillan Publishing Co., Inc. 1968. Reprinted by permission of Macmillan Publishing Co., Inc.

. . . To Ernie, Kelly, Jeff, and the Kents, whose love, patience, and support never wavered.

. . . To the many friends and students who believed in the need.

. . . To Wanda White, without whom it might not have happened.

CONTENTS

AUTHORS' NOTE:
A WORD FROM JOAN AND RICKY

"I CAN'T SING!"

"I can't sing!"

If I've heard those words once, I've heard them hundreds of times. And each time I hear them I cringe inwardly, because I **know** *that ANYONE CAN SING. Except for the very few people who are handicapped by a vocal or auditory disorder, anyone can learn to sing . . . and sing beautifully! Beautiful singing is a physical response that can be learned. By anyone. By you!*

Whenever I meet somebody for the first time and during the course of the conversation they learn that I teach voice at a university, or that I am a professional singer, almost without exception, the following tableau occurs: They snap to attention, their eyes light up, they smile and say, rather wistfully: "Oh, that's interesting. I've always wished I could sing. But, I can't sing!"

Cringe.

"Anyone can sing," says I.

"Not me!" they reply firmly. "You'd never be able to teach **me** *to sing."*

"Do you ever sing?" I'll inquire. "Around the house, or in the shower?"

"Well, yes, but I can't really sing very well."

"Can you reproduce a pitch? Or carry a tune?"

"Yes, but not very well . . . I have no control over my voice. I can't hit any high notes. Sometimes I can't even sing the melody!"

"You **can** *learn to sing," I reiterate. "You can learn to sing because singing is a* **learning** *experience. Anyone can learn to sing!"*

Unfortunately, they are usually not quite convinced. When they read this book (with an open mind) I think they will be!

JOAN WALL

"I CAN SING!"

I remember very clearly my first meeting with Joan and my reaction to learning that she was a professional singer and teacher of voice. My initial reaction was one of awe, followed instantly by the assumption that anyone who earned her living from singing professionally (especially in concert and operatic singing) and who taught other people how to sing, must be a very special kind of person.

My assumption proved to be quite correct. Joan **is** *a special person, but not just because she sings. In retrospect, I have wondered why I felt so awed in the presence of a singer and why I immediately drew the conclusion that an accomplished singer must be an extraordinary person.*

Perhaps the answer is as simple as that a singer's medium is the vital, beautiful, "magical" medium of music. And that a professional singer is one who shares with other musicians in making a personal expression of energy and emotion in music. The singer appears before crowds of other people with the power to entertain them and to elicit an energetic and emotional response from them.

All of this is part of the answer, perhaps—the magic of music, the making of an intensely personal expression in song, the power to touch other people and engender strong responses in them. But it may be only part of the answer because, in actuality, a singer only does what everyone has the potential to do: he sings. Everyone has a voice. But not everyone uses it to sing.

I have discovered that many people don't sing because they think they can't (while often wishing that they could!). Therefore, when they encounter someone who does sing and who derives great pleasure from singing, they greet the singer with awe and find him to be very special. Singers actually do what many people would like very much to do. They sing!

It is my earnest hope that our book will help people to know that indeed they can sing and that they can learn to sing better. I am eager for everyone to discover (as I finally did) the freedom and pleasure of using their own voice to make the satisfying personal expression in music called **singing!**

RICKY WEATHERSPOON

INTRODUCTION

EVALUATING YOUR VOICE

AND ITS POTENTIAL

Before you begin to read ANYONE CAN SING, take up a pen or pencil and spend a few minutes evaluating the *present status* of your *speaking* and *singing voice*. We ask you to evaluate both your speech and singing voice because SPEECH IS VERY CLOSELY RELATED TO SINGING. Even though you may not believe right now that you can sing, the very fact that you use your voice effectively every day in speech means that you have already established the framework for singing successfully. We also ask you to evaluate how you feel about your potential for singing successfully in the future.

The purpose of filling out the following charts is only to assess how you feel *right now* about *your voice* and its *potential for improvement*. After you read ANYONE CAN SING, we will ask you to reconsider your analysis. It will be interesting to see if any changes occur in your self-evaluation after you have read the entire book and performed the exercises according to directions.

As a rating guideline for the charts, consider that on a scale of 0 to 100, a rating of 100 per cent indicates a voice that is as beautiful, effective, and expressive as a voice can be. At the opposite extreme, a 0 per cent rating indicates a voice that is totally ineffective, weak, and unattractive. Most people will rate themselves somewhere in between.

My Speaking Voice

My speaking voice is excellent; there is no way
I could improve it.   _____   100% Perfect

My speaking voice is sufficiently developed   _____   90%
that I can communicate with subtlety and
power of expression.   _____   80%

My speaking voice is quite attractive and   _____   70%
effective.
                                                                    _____   60%

My speaking voice is average. It meets my
needs in daily communication.   _____   50% Average

                                                                    _____   40%

My speaking voice is ineffective; it needs
considerable improvement.   _____   30%

                                                                    _____   20%

                                                                    _____   10%

My speaking voice is completely ineffective.   _____   0% Totally
                                                                             Inadequate

My Singing Voice

My singing voice is excellent; there is no way
I could improve it. _____ 100% Perfect

_____ 90%

My singing voice is sufficiently developed that
I can create outstanding musical expressions. _____ 80%

_____ 70%

My singing voice is quite attractive and
effective. _____ 60%

My singing voice is average. _____ 50% Average

_____ 40%

My singing voice is ineffective; it needs
considerable improvement. _____ 30%

_____ 20%

_____ 10%

My singing voice is completely ineffective. _____ 0% Totally
Inadequate

My Potential for Future Success in Singing

How do you rate the POSSIBILITY of your achieving singing success in the future (i.e., singing songs beautifully and effectively)? This is not being asked to determine whether you actually want to perform or to seek a professional career. But, IF you DID want to, what do you think your chances would be for success?

I could do anything with my voice. I could be as good as the most accomplished professional singer.	_____	100% Perfect
I could sing well enough to be a successful professional singer.	_____	90%
I could sing successfully in semiprofessional local productions.	_____	80%
I could sing solos effectively in amateur groups. I could be a strong choir member.	_____	70%
	_____	60%
I could participate comfortably and securely in group singing.	_____	50% Average
I could learn to sing well enough for my own pleasure and really enjoy it.	_____	40%
	_____	30%
I could learn to sing better, but still not very well; not always on pitch; couldn't learn to carry a tune flawlessly.	_____	20%
	_____	10%
I couldn't sing at all. I couldn't learn. There's no hope for improvement.	_____	0% Totally Inadequate

ANYONE CAN SING

CHAPTER ONE

IF YOU FEEL LIKE SINGING, SING!

———————————— ❊ ❊ ❊ ————————————

RAGS TO RICHES

Even as far back as the 1930s, it was recognized that the old misconception about a good singing voice being limited to a very few who possess special endowments should be corrected by promulgating an "everybody can sing" policy in the vocal teaching profession. More than forty years ago, vocal authority Homer George Mowe wrote that "good singing depends on the proper USE of the voice rather than on some 'extra part' in the throat of the singer that the nonsinger does not possess." Therefore, he continued, "We know and can say with authority that *any normal person can develop a good singing voice.*"

Rags to riches . . . the familiar story of a humbly born young performer whose brilliant natural talent is discovered accidentally, and just in the nick of time, by a kindly maestro/talent scout/producer/director who catapults the talented youngster into instant fame and fortune . . . a classic Hollywood myth.

Remember the movies where such film stars as Judy Garland, Mario Lanza, Mickey Rooney, Doris Day, Frank Sinatra, and Jane Powell made us believe time and time again that glorious things await the fortunate few who somehow emerged from the womb with their natural talents intact, ready, and waiting to serenade the world?

It was superb entertainment. Marvelous fantasy. Grand fun. But it wasn't true to life.

In reality, every talent—whether it is for business, sport, art, singing, whatever—must be developed by plain old-fashioned hard work and training. Although some people seem to be born with special aptitudes which enable them to capitalize on their basic talents and eventually excel in their chosen endeavor, it is a mistake to believe that their excellence was achieved instantaneously. It wasn't! They worked for it. They set themselves a goal, dedicated themselves toward achieving it, and—if they persevered—they achieved.

Consider any outstanding person in any given field. They didn't get there overnight. They worked for it. They sacrificed for it. They dedicated themselves toward achieving it. They believed in themselves. They persevered. And with a little bit of luck, they accomplished their goal. Providing, of course, that their goal was realistic. No matter how fast I flap my arms, I'll never fly.

Anyone can do anything he really wants to do if he is willing to expend the effort it takes to learn how to do it. Singers are not born. They are made. Some people do have a particular aptitude for singing, apparent from the time they are very young. If they are fortunate, and if this aptitude is nourished, their musical abilities will develop and grow . . . simply through assimilating healthy musical learning experiences within a supportive environment. Thus, they can achieve precocious musicianship at a tender age.

If, on the other hand, this very same person (the one with a special aptitude for singing) is *not* supported, if his musical proclivity is frowned upon, if he is not encouraged to develop, if his fledgling musical expressions are thwarted and unrewarding, he can be programmed into thinking and believing that he *can't* sing. In spite of the fact that he has an aptitude for singing!

Most of us fall into the vast in-between category which is bordered at one extreme by those persons with a special aptitude for singing, and at the other extreme by those few who are handicapped by special problems that prohibit them from singing. I am talking here about people who suffer from an organic difficulty (such as deafness or cleft palate) or the *rare* hearing problem of not being able to match a pitch. Such people are very few in number. In all my experience as a voice teacher, working with hundreds of students, I have encountered only one person, a man, who was truly tone deaf.

Everyone else, including YOU, can learn to sing beautifully! All you have to do is *do it!*

USING YOUR VOICE

Because singing involves sound, the logical place to begin is by making sounds, instead of just reading about sound-making. Therefore, the next part of this chapter is devoted to a series of ten vocal exercises that illustrate the ease with which attractive singing sounds can be produced. The exercises also help to warm up your vocal muscles, much in the same way an athlete or dancer warms up his muscles. *Don't just read* the exercises . . . *do them aloud*. It's the *doing aloud* that counts!

The purpose of the many exercises which we will intersperse throughout the book is to convince you that ANYONE CAN SING and that anyone can learn to sing *better*. The purpose of the exercises is not to teach you to become a polished, professional singer. Learning to sing to the very best of your potential would require lessons from a good voice teacher because demonstration, feedback, and corrected responses are necessary in order to achieve ultimate vocal progress. Although voice lessons are necessary in learning to sing your best, learning to sing better can be accomplished *on your own*. These exercises will help you sing better!

Perform Exercises 1 through 10 straight through, without interruption. Follow all directions carefully and do the exercises the suggested number of times (or more times if you wish!). Above all, don't just *read* the exercises . . . do them *out loud!*

VOCAL EXERCISE 1

Let's begin with a soothing chant-like sound. Repeat the following on one note, using any pitch that is a comfortable speaking pitch for you. You will probably find a low note to be more comfortable. This sound is "oh," as in the words "h*o*me," "*o*ak," or "*o*kay."

Say: Ohm.
Use lots of "m." Ohm-m-m-m-m-m-m.
Say it SOFTLY, making the "m" feel buzzy, buzzy.
Ohm-m-m-m-m-m-m.

You are sustaining a speaking sound. (Singing is an extension of speech!) When saying the "m," feel the vibrations of sound near your lips.

Ohm-m-m-m-m-m-m.   Ohm-m-m-m-m-m-m.   Ohm-m-m-m-m-m-m.

Be careful not to clench your jaw. Drop your jaw a little, slightly separating your teeth on the "m" while keeping your lips closed. Let the sound vibrate, be buzzy. Repeat the Ohm a few more times.

Ohm-m-m-m-m-m-m.   Ohm-m-m-m-m-m-m.   Ohm-m-m-m-m-m-m.

SPECIAL NOTE: *The tip of your tongue should be touching the back of your bottom front teeth.*

Repeat three more times. Relax, allowing the sound to flow easily.

Ohm-m-m-m-m-m-m.   Ohm-m-m-m-m-m-m.   Ohm-m-m-m-m-m-m.

Repeat again, this time a little louder. Take a deeper breath before each Ohm. Listen to the vibrating, louder sound. Enjoy the slow, repetitive rhythm. Relax.

Ohm-m-m-m-m-m-m.   Ohm-m-m-m-m-m-m.   Ohm-m-m-m-m-m-m.

VOCAL EXERCISE 2

Now say Ohm again, but this time change the exercise slightly by lengthening the initial vowel sound. Sustain the "oh" longer. Sit or stand comfortably, without allowing your chest to cave in. A sunken chest restricts breathing.

Oh _____ m _____ m.

Oh _____ m _____ m.

Oh _____ m _____ m.

Be sure you are saying the vowel sound "oh" as in the words "home" or "oak." The "oh" should now be sustained for TWO full seconds and the "m" for FOUR full seconds.

To discover the length of one second say the words, "one-thousand-one." Feel the rhythm in your mind and body.

ONE-THOUSAND-ONE	ONE-THOUSAND-TWO	ONE-THOUSAND-THREE	etc.
(EQUALS)	(EQUALS)	(EQUALS)	
1 SECOND	2 SECONDS	3 SECONDS	etc.

Oh _____ m _____ m.

Repeat three times. You may need to take in a deeper breath. Allow the "m" sound to vibrate freely . . . don't force out the sound. The "m" should be gentle.

VOCAL EXERCISE 3

Repeat Ohm, this time sustaining "oh" for FOUR full seconds and "m" also for FOUR seconds. Sustain a single pitch of your own choice. Do not allow the pitch to change while sustaining the Ohm.

Oh _____ m _____ m.

Oh _____ m _____ m.

Oh _____ m _____ m.

Take a deeper breath, but stay very relaxed in your shoulders and neck. Close your eyes and say three more Ohms.

Oh _____ m _____ m.
Oh _____ m _____ m.
Oh _____ m _____ m.

VOCAL EXERCISE 4

Using the same comfortable chanting mood you have established with Ohm, sing the first line of the familiar song "Row Your Boat." Sing only the first phrase of the song. Sing slowly.

ROW, ROW, ROW YOUR BOAT.
ROW, ROW, ROW YOUR BOAT.
ROW, ROW, ROW YOUR BOAT.

Repeat over and over again, while sitting comfortably in your chair, staying very relaxed. Sing only the first line of the song. Do not make the pronunciation of "boat" jerky. Sustain it about as long as the word "row."

ROW, ROW, ROW YOUR BOAT.
ROW, ROW, ROW YOUR BOAT.
ROW, ROW, ROW YOUR BOAT.

Sit up straighter in the chair. Breathe more deeply. Repeat. Make the melody smooth, connected, not jerky or percussive. It should be almost monotonous, like a chant or a lullaby. Breathe only at the end of the third line.

ROW, ROW, ROW YOUR BOAT.
ROW, ROW, ROW YOUR BOAT.
ROW, ROW, ROW YOUR BOAT.   (Breathe)

VOCAL EXERCISE 5

Now, instead of singing the words *Row, row, row your boat,* sing the syllables *ohm, ohm, ohm, ohm, ohm* to the tune of the first line of the song.

Example:

Sing slowly

Instead of
Singing: Row, row, row your boat; Row, row, row   your boat; Row, row, row your boat.

Sing this: Ohm, ohm, ohm, ohm, ohm, ohm, ohm, ohm, ohm, ohm, ohm, ohm, ohm, ohm, ohm.

Repeat several times. Use lots of "m-m-m."

You are producing a singing sound. If you find it pleasing, continue with the next exercises.

If you don't like the sound, simply begin over again with Exercise 1 and Ohm-m-m-m-m-m-m and search for a sound that is pleasing to you. Everyone is capable of making many different kinds of sounds. Experiment. Find one that *feels easy* and that you like.

In our society today, success is often equated with the speed of learning, but singing is an exception to this characteristic of contemporary life. The goal in singing is simply to make sustained sounds that are pleasing to yourself and perhaps even to others. It doesn't matter if this takes a day, a week, a month, or even a year. The goal is to produce pleasant sustained sounds. When you achieve that, it makes not one bit of difference how long or short a time it took you to do it. The fact is . . . you did it! The process of learning to sing is an enjoyable one and you will continue to sing better and better.

After listening to your Ohm, it may surprise you to discover that you are sustaining an attractive sound. The sustained "m" at the end of the word Ohm is a *hum*. When you sustain the word Ohm, you are no longer speaking . . . you are singing. Sustained speech becomes singing. If you hum a melody, you are singing that melody!

VOCAL EXERCISE 6

Hum the first phrase of "Row Your Boat" three times, without stopping to pause or take additional breath between phrases. Take in enough air to sing one long, continuous line.

Example:

Instead of
Singing: Row, row, row your boat; Row, row, row   your boat; Row, row, row   your boat.(Breathe)
Hum: m ———————————————————————————————————————.(Breathe)

Repeat three times.

VOCAL EXERCISE 7

1. Repeat Ohm as you did in Exercise 3. Sustain "oh" for four seconds and "m" for four seconds. Remember to keep the "m" buzzy.

   Oh _____ m _____ m.
   Oh _____ m _____ m.
   Oh _____ m _____ m.

2. Change the vowel sound "oh" to "aw." This is the same sound as the initial vowel sound in the words *"awe"* or *au*tumn." Keep the same long sustained sounds, as with Ohm.

   Aw _____ m _____ m.
   Aw _____ m _____ m.
   Aw _____ m _____ m.

Keep the vocal tone smooth and even, not pulsing or jerky. Remember to sing the word Awm on a single pitch . . . that is, do not let the pitch slide up or down while you are sustaining the word.

   Aw _____ m _____ m.
   Aw _____ m _____ m.
   Aw _____ m _____ m.

Repeat three times on a *higher* pitch. Keep the tip of the tongue touching the back of the bottom front teeth.

   Aw _____ m _____ m.
   Aw _____ m _____ m.
   Aw _____ m _____ m.

Repeat three times on a *lower* pitch.

Aw _____ m _____ m.

Aw _____ m _____ m.

Aw _____ m _____ m.

If you find yourself becoming aware of mouth positions (such as the shape of the lips, how much space is involved inside the mouth, where the tongue is) or of the ease with which you can do these exercises, or of the feeling of vibrations, that is significant. Physical self-awareness is an important factor in singing.

3. Now drop your jaw, relax your lips, and change the vowel to "ah." This is the same sound as in the word "*father*" or "*box*." Use any pitch.

Ah _____ m _____ m.

Ah _____ m _____ m.

Ah _____ m _____ m.

4. Change the vowel to "ee" as in the word "*beet*."

Ee _____ m _____ m.

Ee _____ m _____ m.

Ee _____ m _____ m.

VOCAL EXERCISE 8

Sing the entire song "Row Your Boat" on any pitch that is comfortable for you.

ROW YOUR BOAT

The purpose of this exercise is to make attractive singing sounds in a song. If the song seems easy to sing, just listen to your sound and try to maintain the free, easy quality you experienced on Ohm.

If the top note, on the third phrase of the poem (Merrily), seems strained or difficult, sing it *softer*.

Consciously develop an attitude of pleasure. Imagine yourself drifting down a stream in a boat, daydreaming, fishing, rowing. Sing this song for your own entertainment while you and your boat drift down the stream. Now, in your imagination, hear the song wafting across the water from a long distance. It may be the echo of your own singing, or perhaps the song is coming from someone in another, distant boat. Sing . . . imitating the sound of that faraway song.

> Row, row, row your boat,
> Gently down the stream.
> Merrily, merrily, merrily, merrily,
> Life is but a dream.

Next, imagine another boat passing yours with a group of people singing the song happily and vigorously. Now YOU sing it with that same sound . . . loud and happy.

> Row, row, row your boat,
> Gently down the stream.
> Merrily, merrily, merrily, merrily,
> Life is but a dream.

Use your imagination vividly and the quality of your singing will change.

You may have sung slower and chosen a different pitch for the soft, faraway singing from the one you used for the boisterous, happy singing. When you use imagination in the production of a song, you are being creative musically.

VOCAL EXERCISE 9

Instead of singing the words *Row, row, row your boat,* sing the syllable *Ohm, Ohm, Ohm, Ohm, Ohm* to the tune of the entire song. Breathe only where indicated by the symbol (B).

Example:

Use lots of "m." Be sure you are singing Ohm this time, not Awm or Ahm or any other variation. Sit tall in your chair and breathe deeply. Or stand tall and remain alert. Repeat the song three times.

VOCAL EXERCISE 10

HUM the entire song. Remember a hum is just the "m" of Ohm. It feels and sounds buzzy.

Your aim is to accomplish a free, easy, flowing sound. It will help if you separate your teeth, thereby relaxing your jaw. Pretending that you have a couple of marbles in your mouth will help the sound become more buzzy. Hum the entire song again. Your lips should remain closed.

m ——————————— etc . . . .

The sound remains very vibrating and buzzy. Hum the melody again, but this time start on a different pitch (higher or lower).

m ——————————— etc . . . .

WARNING!

It may be tempting at this point to peek ahead and experiment with subsequent exercises . . . but it is important to resist the temptation! If the exercises are not performed in sequence, and within the context of the supplementary informational material, you will not derive the full benefits from the exercises and you will not fully convince yourself of your own capabilities.

MORE SELF-EVALUATION

After you have completed Exercises 1 through 10, fill out the next VOICE EVALUATION CHART. The purpose of this chart is for you to evaluate—as honestly and as objectively as you possibly can—your present speaking and singing voice. Place a checkmark in the NOW column of the chart, alongside all of the words that best describe your present speaking and singing voice. Then go back and place a checkmark in the GOAL column to indicate how you would like your voice to sound. This helps to establish your ultimate goal in speech and singing by identifying the kind of speaking and singing voice that you would like to possess.

VOICE EVALUATION CHART

Place a checkmark (√) in the NOW column alongside the words that best describe your PRESENT speaking and singing voice. Then place a second checkmark in the GOAL column to indicate how you would LIKE your voice to sound.

	SPEAKING		SINGING				SPEAKING		SINGING	
QUALITY	Now	Goal	Now	Goal			Now	Goal	Now	Goal
1 Pleasant						30 Strident				
2 Sweet						31 Harsh				
3 Warm						32 Hoarse				
4 Tender						33 Nasal				
5 Sexy						34 Breathy				
6 Masculine						35 Uneven				
7 Feminine						36 Strained				
8 Calm						37 Rough				
9 Sincere						38 Raspy				
10 Secure						39 Gravelly				
11 Confident						40 Sharp				
12 Clear						41 Shaky				
13 Smooth						42 Tremulous				
14 Deep										
15 Rich						**LOUDNESS**				
16 Expressive										
17 Powerful						1 Appropriate				
18 Weak						2 Too loud				
19 Timid						3 Too soft				
20 Apologetic										
21 Insincere						**PITCH**				
22 Nervous										
23 Cold						1 Appropriate				
24 Aggressive						2 Melodious				
25 Abrasive						3 Interesting				
26 Ugly						4 Limited range				
27 Raucous						5 Too high				
28 Thin						6 Too low				
29 Throaty						7 Monotonous				
						8 Singsongy				
						9 Dull				

TEMPO	SPEAKING		SINGING		DICTION	SPEAKING		SINGING	
	Now	Goal	Now	Goal		Now	Goal	Now	Goal
1 Appropriate					1 Appropriate				
2 Too fast					2 Inappropriate				
3 Too slow					3 Clear				
					4 Pretentious				
					5 Clipped				
BREATH					6 Muffled				
1 Easy					7 Sloppy				
2 Sufficient					8 Good				
3 Insufficient					9 Poor				
4 Obtrusive									
5 Labored									
6 Noisy									

IF YOU FEEL LIKE SINGING, SING!

We titled our first chapter, "If You Feel Like Singing, Sing!" because it is a phrase that comes very close to summarizing our philosophy about singing. Not only *can* anyone sing, but if they feel like singing, they *should* sing.

Singing is an energizing physical act that is self-satisfying, entertaining, and provides a socially acceptable outlet for releasing our emotions. When we feel so happy that we simply cannot contain ourselves, we can jump for joy and burst into song (just like they do in the movies!).

If you feel like screaming . . . SING!

Since screaming, dish-breaking, people-punching, and various other sorts of mayhem are considered socially unacceptable, perhaps we might try converting our screams and those other volatile energies into song. It would certainly be less expensive than replacing broken dishes!

If you feel lethargic . . . SING!

The act of singing is energizing and uplifting. If we feel apathetic and start to sing, we will perk up and become more alert and vibrant.

If you feel like having fun . . . SING!

Singing is fun because it involves music. When we listen to music we like, it makes us feel good. When we become a participator (by singing) and actually create music we like, it makes us feel better. Even our muscles react involuntarily to the rhythm of music. No one can truly listen to rousing music without tapping his toe, nodding his head, snapping his fingers, or clapping his hands.

Singing is also fun when it becomes a social activity. There is a special kind of pleasure and feeling of identity among the kindred spirits who sing together in choruses, local musical productions, barbershop quartets, church congregations, around a campfire, at a piano bar, or even just harmonizing with a friend.

If you feel like worshiping . . . SING!

Singing is a personal expression of the highest order. The act of singing can be so uplifting as to accomplish a mystical or spiritual experience. The act of singing in a congregational circumstance unites individuals in a spiritual togetherness.

If you want to feel good . . . SING!

Music satisfies and contributes to our sense of well-being because music is the ultimate organizer and our bodies respond to its order. Because singing is an expression of music, it involves musical elements such as rhythm, melody, and harmony, all of which have positive emotional and physical effects upon us. People consciously use music to complement *or* to actually help change their emotions. Some people, when they are feeling blue, play sad music; others, when they feel sad, play happy music. Whether we use music to reflect our mood or to help change it, the music provides an emotional catharsis that improves our feeling of well-being.

If you want to grow . . . SING!

Singing promotes personal growth in numerous ways. It helps us become more expressive, improves posture, improves our speaking voice and diction, improves our interpretive sense by stimulating a deeper understanding of the words of the song, develops character by improving self-discipline, and strengthens memory and powers of concentration (in learning new songs). Singing even contributes to better health by promoting deep breathing, which develops the lungs and purifies the blood.

Perhaps the single most important benefit derived from singing is that it promotes a greater interest in music. And music helps us "stay alive" instead of withering on the vine. It helps us keep in touch with our emotions, even emotions that we may have repressed.

If you want to remain vital . . . SING!

Singing songs keeps us vital because we experience energizing pleasure while singing familiar old songs and intellectual stimulation while learning new ones. It improves the quality of life abundantly. Besides providing a constructive emotional outlet that removes inhibitions and releases tensions, singing makes us more aware of our total body energy and body language. It helps us become more effective and expressive communicators.

Singing belongs to you and to me for both of us to use to create music. Music affects us powerfully. It is an emotional language that is around us all the time. It is affecting us all the time. Through singing we have a method for expressing its constructive effects. Let's use it!

CHAPTER TWO

THE THREE "E'S" . . .
ENERGY, EMOTION, EXPRESSION

* * *

"THE BEST THING"

Getting into singing was the best thing that ever happened to me!
JOAN WALL

What I mean by "the best thing that ever happened" is that singing eventually led to my careers as a performer, teacher, and writer, all of which have brought me enormous pleasure, happiness, fulfillment, and satisfaction. But singing meant considerably more than the significance it had upon the direction of my life. Singing also enriched the **quality** *of my life, immeasurably. It was indelibly intertwined with my growth as a person.*

Singing involves not only music and adequate musical expression, it involves **personal** *expression. It deals with a revealing of one's self. This I believe to be a primary source of the appeal and value of singing. It is an acceptable outlet for expressing ourselves socially as we interact with others, and it allows us a private expression of emotion and energy when we are alone. In singing, whether we sing for ourselves only, or for ourselves and others, we become involved in the emotional language that is unique to music. We get in touch with our emotions, we feel them, we express them, and we experience aesthetic and cathartic pleasure in releasing them.*

There is something about singing that sets it apart from any other form of musical expression and that gives it a special appeal to almost everyone . . . whether we are actually doing it or listening to it. Perhaps this is because singing is an ultimate personal experience that combines the profuse orderliness and supremely emotive language of music and words with the personal expression of the energy and emotion of self. Our voice is part of ourselves. Singing is an intensely personal communication of our self.

I believe that people sing because they have a desire to express themselves in music, or they want to experience the pure joy of singing, or they need and enjoy the rewards of the glamour and acclaim accorded to the successful performance of song. All of these—music, expression, joy, singing, glamour, acclaim—imply emotion, exhilaration, vitality, energy.

Music is sound that is put together in such a way that it creates and expresses emotion and energy. The rhythm, intensity, and tempo of every piece of music are a reflection of the energy and emotion of its composer. In a song, the singer takes the creative product of a composer and brings it to life through his interpretive expression of the energy and emotion inherent in the song. Not only does he express the energy and emotion of the song as delineated by the composer, the singer also expresses his own personal energy and emotion as well. **When the energy and emotion of the composer and the singer are in synchrony, singing actually becomes easier and the voice sounds better!**

It seems to me that the containment and release of energy is basic to all of life and to every activity. I know that it is absolutely basic to singing. For this reason, we will spend considerable time in ANYONE CAN SING discovering the relationship between energy and singing and using energy as a vehicle for singing better.

In addition to answering the question whether anyone can sing (They can!), this book contains information about the aesthetics, techniques, and benefits of singing, about the musical relationship between speech and singing, and about the elements of music and song. You will discover that there is an underlying, basic factor that links all of this material together. That one factor is energy. And that is where we shall begin . . . with **energy** *and its inseparable companion,* **emotion.**

JOAN

ENERGY AND EMOTION

The science of physics tells us that energy is the capacity for doing work and overcoming inertia. Energy is not the work itself; it is the capacity for doing that work. Energy is not power; it is the potential power which exists prior to being released.

The energy of every song and every piece of music is expressed in its RHYTHM, TEMPO, and INTENSITY, which combine together to create a life force that is the source of its unique musical flow, vitality, power, communication, and expression. Likewise, every person has energy which is expressed through the contraction and relaxation of his muscles. In human behavior, the potential power (energy) is released in the rhythm, tempo, and intensity of muscular action. RHYTHM refers to the *patterns* of musical notes and human activities; TEMPO, to their *speed* of performance; and IN-TENSITY, to their particular *degree* of loudness, tension, or thrust.

In music, emotion is derived from the energy of the music and the usage and arrangement of the basic elements of which music is composed. (These basic musical elements are rhythm, tempo, pitch, dynamics, harmony, tone color, and form. They will be defined and discussed at length in Chapter Four.) In a song, emotion is derived from its energy, its usage of musical elements, and its text. The derivation of emotion in humans poses a difficult problem because the question of the source of intangible human emotion is a philosophical one. We do know, however, that there is a direct correlation between emotion and the method in which energy is released physically. Getting in touch with a specific type of energy release enables us to get in touch with a specific emotion. Further, if we change the way in which energy is released, we can alter our attitudinal state; conversely, a deliberate change of emotion results in a corresponding change in the release of energy.

Because singing is a musical, physical, and emotional expression, a singer discovers an exhilarating sense of "rightness" and pleasure when he synchronizes the release of the energy and emotion of the song with the way in which he releases his personal energy and emotion. When he achieves this identity and balance between the song and its expression, he experiences physical and psychical freedom and, subsequently, a surprising ease of vocal production. For this reason, every beginning singer needs to learn and to get in touch with the energy and emotion of the song, and then to concentrate upon expressing the essence of the song. The essence of the song is what the song is . . . its form and content; its rhythm, tempo, and intensity; its emotion and energy.

ENERGY IS BASIC TO EVERYTHING

Energy, as seen in rhythm, cycles, vibration, and order, pervades every aspect of life and nature. Everything in the universe as we know it has its own peculiar beat, its own rhythmic pulse, its own shape and design, its own cosmic order. Rhythm is found in the structure of time (seconds, minutes, hours, days, years) and in the passage of time (the coming and going of the seasons). Every form of life—vegetable, insect, animal, and human—experiences the rhythmic cycles of birth, growth, death.

In addition to the larger cycles of life, every living creature has its own smaller basic rhythms. A bee buzzes, a snake undulates, a bird pecks and soars, a small fish zigzags in random directions, a large fish circles and glides, a bug scoots, a rabbit darts, a cat slinks, a hippopotamus lumbers, a giraffe stretches, an elephant plods, a camel sways, a kangaroo hops, a squirrel scurries, a bobcat leaps, a horse walks, prances, gallops. And man? Well, multifarious man does most of the above!

Each person has a unique basic body energy which manifests itself in bodily rhythm, tempo, and tension and pervades our entire behavior . . . movement, speech, singing, thought, everything. Fortunately, we all have different degrees of energy and different ways of releasing it, and this is what makes each of us unique. If it were otherwise, we would all resemble robots.

In this section we will explore the types of energy release patterns that each of us uses in movement, speech, and singing. IDENTIFYING AND UNDERSTANDING THE RELATION OF ENERGY IN MOVEMENT, SPEECH, MUSIC, AND SONG LEADS TO CREATIVE AND EXPRESSIVE SINGING. We begin first by discussing energy in movement because movement is visual and permits an easier, more accurate determination of how energy is released. After a working vocabulary is established and after you actually experience and can identify different kinds of tension and energy release in your own body, you will be better equipped to communicate energy and emotion expressively in song.

ENERGY IN MOVEMENT

Have you ever indulged in the fascinating pastime of "people-watching?" What interesting things people do! But instead of looking at what people do, try examining how they do it, how they move. Their movements will reflect accurately the rhythm, tempo, and release of muscular tension that is characteristic of their basic body energy!

The following classification of the ways in which people express their body energy should help you to recognize the various kinds of energy release and to label them by name. The types of energy release are: VIBRATORY, PERCUSSIVE, STACCATO, SUSTAINED, PENDULAR, LYRICAL, SUSPENDED, and COLLAPSED. They are used singly and in combination. Remember, these same categories also describe the ways in which energy is released in speech, music, and singing.

1. Vibratory

Vibratory describes the kind of energy release which stems from the greatest amount of tension. For example, if you hold your arm straight out from your body while holding a heavy weight (at shoulder height), after a time your muscles will contract rigidly and your hand and arm will begin to vibrate involuntarily. The action of your body, this involuntary quivering and shaking caused by the excessive contraction of muscles, is called "vibratory." The same energy release occurs when people shake involuntarily with fear or anger. As a singing teacher, I observe it in singers whose head, jaw, and tongue shake involuntarily when they employ excessive tension in creating singing tones.

2. Percussive

Percussive release is explosive, powerful, energized, controlled, and has a defined beginning and end. Examples include a slap, punch, karate chop, hammering, vigorous marching.

3. Staccato

A staccato release of energy is sharp and quick, sometimes a series of repeated happenings that are smaller and less explosive than percussive. Examples include flicking water off your wrist, tapping typewriter keys, walking in quick steps, nervous movements, quick movements of the head.

4. Sustained

A sustained release is slow, continuous, growing; usually moving in design and space, but always containing considerable intensity and a sense of growing tension. (Think of a choral conductor who uses great tension in his arms and body to elicit a smooth, slowly building, intense crescendo from his chorus, or think of a man stirring a large vat of glue with a wide stick.) Even in a relatively confined sustained movement, there is a sense of growth because of the stretching and interplay between opposing tensions (such as the action of stretching to pick an apple from a branch that is barely out of reach).

5. Pendular

A pendular release of energy involves a back-and-forth activity such as the movement that occurs when your arms swing at your side while you walk or when you swing your arms back and forth in front of your body while exercising. At the top of the swing, the arm has energy which is released as the downward arc begins. As the arm reaches bottom, you again activate muscle activity and then repeat the pattern of engaging and releasing, etc. Pendular release begins with energy that is released and then regained (as in a waltz).

6. *Lyrical*

The sixth type of energy release is lyrical . . . a flowing, graceful, continuous activity that implies ease of movement. (Lyrical release has considerably less intensity than sustained.) Examples are: Gently stirring water with your hand, fingers open, no feeling of resistance; the flow and continuous tracing of the figure "8" on the ice with your ice skates. In body movements, lyrical often suggests a curved line.

7. *Suspended*

The seventh type of energy release is suspended, which refers to the stillness between activities . . . a hold, a suspension, a pause. In movement, for example, a prior activity is interrupted and then held at the same level of power. The energy of the suspension usually reflects the intensity used in the prior activity, although sometimes it will anticipate a forthcoming one. Suspended refers to the "hold," the suspension of activity, the maintaining of a specific degree of tension that neither grows nor diminishes in intensity.

This type of energy release differs from the others in that a suspension always relates in intensity to another activity; whereas, the seven other types of energy release can function independently. For example, we can make a percussive movement that ends in a suspension, or we can do a lyrical movement that ends in suspension. In both cases, the suspension is an appendage of the prior movement and contains the same degree of muscular tension as the prior movement.

8. *Collapse*

The final type of energy release is the collapse, a complete or partial release of tension, in which all or part of the activity ceases. In a complete collapse of the body, the entire body falls limply to the floor in response to gravitational pull (as in a faint). In a partial collapse, the entire body either regains tension quickly, thus halting the fall, or tension is released in a single part of the body (such as the neck) causing only a portion of the body to fall (such as the head).

The degree of released energy—tension—tends to decrease in intensity from the first type of energy release (vibratory) down to the eighth (collapse). The seventh release (suspended) can vary in intensity.

Carefully observe the people around you, and see if you can identify their movements according to the eight types of energy release. The more you do it, the better you will get at it. After observing someone over a long period of time and under various circumstances, you will find that specific movement patterns begin to emerge. The person you are observing will use one type of energy release, or a specific combination of types, more than he uses the others. This will be his unique basic body energy.

Joe Smoothfellow, for example, has a basic body energy that is clearly *lyrical*. There is a flow and continuousness about him which pervades his entire behavior (when viewed overall). Mr. Smoothfellow, however, is not a pushover. When the occasion demands, he can be very commanding and authoritative. He can pound the table quite percussively at a business meeting to get his point across emphatically; he excels at karate; he dances a spritely polka and a graceful waltz. In other words, there will be times when he expresses all of the other energy types as well as his basic body energy. But when we look at the gestalt, the whole, and examine the general tone of his life movements and expressions, they are lyrical.

A person's basic body energy permeates almost everything he does . . . the way he moves, speaks, sings, and thinks, whether he is asleep or awake, energetic or lethargic, cheerful or angry, feeling good or feeling bad. In keeping with our basic body energy, we all have a characteristic tendency to move, speak, sing, and think in a particular fashion. There will be appropriate times when we deviate from this pattern, but we will return to releasing energy in the mode that is basic and natural to us.

ENERGY IN SPEECH

People speak in recurring rhythmical patterns that correspond to their basic body energy. Rhythm reflects body energy and brings order to speech just as it does to movement and other behaviors. Normal conversational speech is generally consistent in tempo, and the degree of tension generally remains constant. If we combine rhythm patterns, tempo, and tension, speech behavior can also be defined or recognized according to the preceding types of energy release. Jerky speech patterns are "staccato";

smooth patterns, "lyrical"; explosive patterns, "percussive"; singsong patterns, "pendular."

A person's basic body energy sets the stage for his speech patterns. These patterns, in turn, are refined by idiosyncrasies determined by environment, peer groups, education level, family influences, the age (historical period) in which he lives, and by the will of the individual, who can modify his speech if he is motivated strongly enough to change old habits.

The normal tempo of a person's speech can fluctuate extraordinarily according to changes in mood and emotion. In a moment of anxiety or fright, tempo increases and phrases often become jerky. If a person feels safe, comfortable and completely relaxed, the tempo may slow.

Public speakers, politicians, and actors consciously utilize changes in tempo and phrasing to achieve desired effect. This is called "timing." Winston Churchill, one of history's most famous speechmakers, spoke at a moderate to fast rate of speed in normal conversation. But when he spoke before Parliament, or over the radio or on film, he slowed down the tempo of his speech, lengthened the pauses between words, and his audience perked up its ears and listened.

Tempo and rhythm—which both reflect basic body energy—are very closely related in speech. TEMPO is the rate of speech . . . how fast or how slowly we speak. RHYTHM is the organization of sounds into recurring patterns. Rhythm in speech can refer to the overall energy release pattern, and it can refer to smaller units (individual thought units called phrases).

Some people talk fast all the time, while others seem to speak slowly all the time (tempo). Some people never pause long enough to let someone else get a word in edgewise, and others pause so frequently and for such interminable lengths of time that it takes concentrated effort on the part of the listener to pay attention to what is trying to be expressed (rhythm).

Using the sentence "ENERGY IS BASIC TO EVERYTHING IN OUR UNIVERSE," experiment with some of the various ways you can deliberately alter speech rhythm and tempo.

1. Speak the sentence *aloud* as if you can't think of the next word you want to say:
   "Energy . . . is basic . . . to everything . . . in our . . . universe."

2. Say it slowly, pausing for dramatic emphasis:
   "Energy . . . is basic . . . to everything . . . in our universe!"

3. Say it without pausing, as a statement of fact:
   "Energy is basic to everything in our universe."

4. Say it without pausing, as a question:
   "Energy is basic to everything in our universe?"

5. Say it without pausing, as if you are a young child speaking before your

classmates, feeling quite proud of yourself. Try to match a child's youth-
ful vocal quality, using considerable up-and-down inflection:
   "Energy is basic to everything in our universe."

In addition to being aware of variations in rhythm and tempo, you may
also have noticed changes in your volume, inflection (pitch), tone color
(quality of sound), tension, and diction. Actors and politicians are masters
at altering these elements to gain a desired effect.

If you will spend some time observing and concentrating upon the speech
patterns of the people around you, you will become increasingly aware of
individual variations in tempo and rhythm. It is interesting to observe natural speech patterns, bearing in mind that they reflect basic body energy. It is
also interesting to observe the ways in which people consciously vary their
basic speech patterns in order to achieve emphasis and effect. Shakespeare
knew what he was talking about when he wrote: "All the world's a stage,
And all the men and women merely players."

ENERGY IN SINGING

There lies within each of us "players" a deep and abiding yearning to
communicate fully and expressively with others. This very basic need is
fulfilled primarily through the medium of speech, but it is heightened in the
medium of singing because singing is a musical expression in which the energy and emotion of speech are amplified in rhythm, tempo, and intensity.

The fact that singing involves music (and that a musical statement is
larger than life) implies that a person must relate to his own energy and
emotion even more precisely in singing than he does in speech. Further-
more, in addition to being aware of his own energy and emotion, a singer
must also consider the energy and emotion of the song, because every song
is a reflection of its composer. An honest, successful, sincere performance of
a song occurs only after the singer has established a synchronization between
his own energy and emotion and that of the song. Such performances elicit
strong, positive responses from listeners even when the singing is primitive.
A sense of "rightness" prevails, and both the singer and his listeners know
intuitively that the energy and emotion of the singer and the song have become one.

If two people have drastically different basic body energy types, they will
have a natural tendency to sing the same song quite differently. The
differences would be noticeable in their degree of emphasis within the
melodic line, in the manner in which they sing *legato* (a smooth vocal
line), in *volume* (loudness or softness), in *intensity* (the energetic involve-

ment of the sounds), in the attack and release of sounds, in the length of their phrases, in the manner of handling words, and in the way they breathe.

Although we have a tendency to sing a song in keeping with our basic body energy, it does not preclude our ability to adjust innate tendencies in order to meet the requirements of a song. Singers are called upon frequently to make adjustments to the musical energy established by a composer. Some singers are able to accomplish this instinctively; others learn to respond to the rhythm, tempo, and intensity of the music, allowing themselves to merge the energy of music with their own body energy and subsequently express it in their singing. This is called "getting in touch with the music."

Every musical selection, when considered in its totality, is characterized in performance by a basic musical energy. A lullaby, for example, is clearly pendular; a brisk march is percussive; tender ballads are often lyrical; hard rock music is intensely percussive; religious music tends to be lyrical or sustained. In addition to manifesting an overall basic energy, almost every piece of music incorporates in its various sections and parts any, or all, of the other types of energy release. This accounts for the fact that the basic energy of an orchestral work may be sustained when viewed overall, while containing various moments that are lyrical, staccato, suspended, percussive, vibratory, and pendular, for purposes of contrast, balance, and effect. We often find that music is structured in such a way that different instruments simultaneously display entirely different types of energy release. The violins, for example, may be playing agitated staccato notes at exactly the same time the brass instruments play a very sustained legato melody.

A song, then, may have a basic musical energy that is lyrical when considered in its entirety, but within the structure of that song there may be times when it exhibits clearly the other types of energy release as well. When we listen to music for the purpose of trying to "get in touch with the music" (by identifying its types of energy release), we must consider both its overall basic energy and the energies of its various parts.

As you come to understand your own basic body energy, as you get in touch with the energy of music, and as you learn to move more freely, you will find that singing becomes easier and more vital. This next series of exercises is designed to help you sing better by making physical responses to music, thus LOOSENING UP YOUR BODY (of which the vocal instrument is a part) and also helping you to become more free to sing.

The exercises build progressively one upon the other and will help you to understand and relate to the energy and emotion in music. In addition, they will encourage you to make physical and emotional responses to music and to stimulate your creative imagination. AS THE MIND AND BODY BECOME MORE FREE AND MORE RESPONSIVE TO MUSIC, THE

FREEDOM TO MAKE A REWARDING EXPRESSION IN SINGING INCREASES TENFOLD. These exercises will help you to begin to sing and to begin to sing better.

First we ask you to select a piece of recorded music that you really enjoy listening to. Instrumental music that does not have an overly strong melody is best-suited to these exercises. Listen to the music and allow yourself to become absorbed in its energy and emotion. Let it fill you, soothe, inspire, chase away your cares.

Then perform Exercises 2 through 5 and allow yourself to be imaginative. Experiment. Let yourself go. And most important of all . . . relax and enjoy the energetic and emotive language of music. As your mind and body relax and become more free, you will discover that you sing better. SINGING IS A PHYSICAL ACT THAT IS DIRECTLY INFLUENCED BY THE STATE OF TENSIONS AND THE MUSCULAR ACTIVITIES OF THE ENTIRE BODY.

EXERCISE 1

PURPOSE: Loosen up the body.
Become more aware of various parts of the body.
Co-ordinate body movement to music.

Select a piece of recorded music in *duple* or ¾ time, the normal rhythm of most dance music. You can discover whether the music is in duple time by walking in time with the music. If you are on the same foot each time you reach a strong pulse in the music, it is duple time. *Triple* time is a typical waltz rhythm and is not suited to this exercise.

Before beginning, it might be helpful to read through the exercise and familiarize yourself with the various movements before you start doing them to music. Remember that it is possible to move on part of the body while keeping the rest of the body still. Check yourself in a mirror to see if you are moving only the individual part of the body specified in the directions. Then do the movements in time to the music.

1. **HEAD** (each move gets one count)
   Instructions: When moving the head forward, put the chin on chest. When moving the head sideways, pretend you are putting the head on a pillow. Don't lift your shoulder. When head is moved back, feel a stretch under the chin.
   a. Move head forward, right, back, left.
      Move head in opposite direction: forward, left, back, right.
   b. Repeat sequence: To the right, then to the left.

2. SHOULDERS

Instructions: Move only the prescribed shoulder and no other part of the body such as the ribs, hips, or head.

a. Move right shoulder.

   1. Up, 4 times

   2. Forward, 4 times

   3. Backward, 4 times

   4. In a circle, starting forward, 4 times

   5. In a circle, starting backward, 4 times

b. Move left shoulder using same sequence of movements.

c. Move both shoulders simultaneously using same sequence of movements.

3. RIB CAGE

Instructions: This part of the exercise requires you to move your ribs separately from the other parts of your body. If it seems difficult (it does to many people), pretend someone has just stuck you in the left side with a finger . . . your rib cage will move to the right reflexively. To move to the back, imagine a jab in the front of your rib cage. Keep body and head erect.

Your shoulders will move some with this exercise, but the movement should ORIGINATE AT THE RIBS. Keep hips still.

a. Move ribs.

   1. Right, 4 times

   2. Front, 4 times

   3. Left, 4 times

   4. Back, 4 times

b. Move ribs in a circle.

   1. Starting right, 4 times

   2. Starting left, 4 times

4. HIPS

Instructions: Keep your shoulders still and your feet flat.

a. Move hips.

   1. Right, 4 times

   2. Front, 4 times

   3. Left, 4 times

   4. Back, 4 times

   5. Circle, starting right, 4 times

   6. Circle, starting left, 4 times

5. **FEET**

   Instructions: Lift up your heel, while pressing down firmly on the ball of your foot. Arch your foot and bend your knee. Do NOT move your hips. Then return heel to floor. Your feet should be parallel.

   a. Use right foot, 4 times

   b. Use left foot, 4 times

   c. Use alternating feet, 8 times altogether

   d. Both feet together, 8 times

6. **KNEE ROTATION**

   Instructions: Move knee forward and outward in a circle, starting the movement from the hip. Your heel will lift off the floor.

   a. Rotate right knee, 4 times

   b. Rotate left knee, 4 times

   c. Knee rotation using alternate knees, 8 times altogether

   d. Rotate both knees together in the same direction, 4 times to the right, 4 times to the left.

EXERCISE 2

PURPOSE: Promote a physical response to music.
          Identify the types of energy in movement and music.

Do this exercise in a large room with lots of floor space so you can make expansive movements.

1. Select a piece of recorded music that you enjoy listening to. You may choose any type of music, but instrumental music (without too prominent a melody) will be easier to begin with than vocal music. Select music that has a clearly defined energy. You will continue to use this same music throughout Exercises 3 and 4.

2. Listen to the music repeatedly until you can feel its energy. Let it pulsate through you. Try to feel the music's energy in your muscles. Don't analyze or intellectualize; just sit, lie or stand and let your body begin to respond to the energy of the music. Close your eyes. Surrender yourself to the music.

3. After you feel the energy of the music begin to permeate your body, stand up and let your body move freely in whatever way the music suggests. MOVE. Let yourself go. You are a free spirit! Don't criticize your movements. Just move. Let go. Feel the energy. Express it in movement. Let it happen.

4. After you have expressed the energy of the music in movement, refer to the chart below that categorizes the various types of energy in movement and music.

   a. Select the word which best describes the overall energy of your *music*.

   b. Select the word which best describes the energy of your *movements*.

   c. Are the words the same or different for the music and movements?

   d. If the words are the same, change your movements to contrast with the music.

   e. If the words are not the same, change your movements to match the word description of the music.

Chart of Energy Types

1. VIBRATORY: Activities (such as involuntary shaking or quivering) involving a maximum degree of tension or intensity.
2. PERCUSSIVE: Powerful, explosive activities.
3. STACCATO: Sharp, quick activities; smaller and less intense than percussive.
4. SUSTAINED: Slow, continuous, growing activity involving considerable tension or intensity.
5. PENDULAR: Activity in which energy is released and then regained; swinging back and forth.
6. LYRICAL: Flowing, continuous, graceful, gentle motion.
7. SUSPENDED: A "hold," stillness that maintains a specific degree of tension or intensity that neither grows nor diminishes.
8. COLLAPSE: A complete or partial releasing of tension.

EXERCISE 3

PURPOSE: Vary body movements and gain more body freedom.
Learn the basic elements of creative performance by broadening the movements used in response to the energy of music.

1. Use the same music as in Exercise 2.
2. Move to the music as you did in Exercise 2.
3. Vary your movements by using more parts of your body, separately or in combinations. Let the energy of the music continue to be your guide.

4. All movement has DIRECTION—forward, sideways, backward, up or down. Add various directions to your movements.

5. All movement has LEVELS. Think of levels in terms of the relationship of your body to the floor—lying down on the floor, crouching, sitting, standing, leaping. Add various levels to your movements.

6. Movement has FOCUS. If our eyes are open, we are almost always looking at something, but by focus we mean a look with energy, a deliberate focusing upon something specific or in a specific direction. Abrupt change in focus is often used to gain added interest, a new emphasis or extra dynamic power. Vary the focus of your movements.

EXERCISE 4

PURPOSE: Make vocal sounds in response to the energy and emotion of music.

1. Choose a room where you can have privacy. Play the music you used in Exercises 2 and 3.

2. While listening and moving to the music, let yourself make some VOCAL SOUNDS. Come on . . . it's easy! Express the music's energy in any vocal sound . . . whine, moan, grunt, hum, sigh, whistle, scream, whisper, sing "oo," "ah." Make any sound or combination of sounds that fit the energy of the music.

   Let yourself go. Don't criticize the sounds you make. They don't have to be "pretty." (Don't be a critic!) Just allow the sounds to originate because of your emotional and energetic reactions to the music. It will make you feel good to express sounds that express the energy of the music. If you happen to make sounds that are melodious, harmonious, or beautiful, fine; but basically the aim of this exercise is to produce abstract vocal sounds that reflect the energy and emotion of the music as *you* perceive it.

   If you think you don't want to make a vocal expression, DO IT ANYWAY! If you have to force it out, force it out!

3. Use your personal energy to achieve VOCAL LINE. Sound, like movement, can also have direction or line. Musical sounds are not just isolated punctuation marks; they are connected in some type of energy flow. Repeat your sounds to give CONTINUING AND CONNECTED ENERGY. This will create vocal line!

   You are beginning to make a personal vocal expression in music!

EXERCISE 5

PURPOSE: Produce clearly defined types of energy in song.

1. Think back to Chapter One and the "Row Your Boat" exercise which you sang three ways:

   First, you sang it with your own choice of expression.

   Second, you imitated some soft, faraway singing.

   Third, you imitated the sound of a loud, boisterous group singing nearby.

   What type of energy was displayed in the different ways you sang the same song? Did the type of energy remain constant or did it change?

2. Now sing the song "Row Your Boat" three more times, using the following ways of releasing energy:

   1. Staccato

   2. Percussive

   3. Lyrical

In Chapter One we learned that we can become creative musically by using imagination in the production of a song. Now that you are familiar with the eight basic ways of releasing energy, you have established some parameters to guide your imagination. The more clearly and vividly you can imagine something, the more clearly and vividly you can do it. In singing, clearly defined, distinctive release of energy is the basis of STYLE.

CHAPTER THREE

A MUSICAL INSTRUMENT OF OUR OWN

* * *

"REFLECTIONS ON TAKING VOICE LESSONS"

Shortly after Joan and I conceived the idea of writing this book, it became apparent to both of us that the experience of taking voice lessons would be an extremely valuable one for me. I am the typical nonsinging-type person. All my life I have believed that I can't sing, while wishing with equal fervor that I could! As I write this introduction, I don't yet know what will happen as the lessons progress. Joan says that I will learn to sing beautifully, but I have my doubts. You and I will find out together whether she is right!

RICKY WEATHERSPOON

"OhdearLordwhatamIdoinghere?" perfectly illustrates this terrified person's state of mind regarding voice lesson numero uno.

Taking voice lessons is without a doubt the LAST endeavor that I ever expected to undertake. Piano lessons, dance lessons, writing lessons, swimming lessons, driving lessons, religious-instruction lessons, foreign-language lessons, badminton lessons, bridge lessons, cooking lessons . . . throughout my life I have undertaken lessons ad infinitum *with great aplomb. I even remember taking cello lessons for several weeks (until I grew weary of carrying that enormously unwieldy instrument three quarters of a mile home from school each day).*

This kind of background would lead one to believe that I am quite comfortable with lessons—and I am. Otherwise, I would not have spent so much time, energy, and money in the relentless quest for self-improvement via lessons.

Therefore, it must be the particular kind of lesson—the VOICE LESSON —that fills me so with dread, anxiety, fear, goose bumps, sweaty palms, and a lump in my throat the size of which I am certain will prohibit me from making any sound whatsoever. Actually, I would not be surprised if that lump should become a permanent fixture. Can one sing with a permanent lump in one's throat?

All of my life I have wished that I could sing well; I have admired and even envied anyone who did sing well; and I have always known (with absolute certainty) that I DID NOT SING WELL. Until meeting Joan and becoming a convert and proselytizer of her "ANYONE CAN SING" philosophy, I never suspected that there was the ghost of a chance that one day I might be able to learn to sing well. I never considered it.

This new possibility, this new door that is going to open for me, is wonderfully exciting. Why, then, am I scared witless? I, who will tackle almost anything without a moment's hesitation, am as nervous as the proverbial long-tailed cat in a room full of rocking chairs. And I don't understand the reasons why.

I love music. All kinds of music. It plays a big part in my life. I listen to music all the time. I sing in the shower (off-key). I have sung in choruses (always standing next to a strong singer so they could show me the way). But the thought of singing solo in front of somebody (even Joan, whom I know well) is devastating.

The only rationale for this state of mind was mentioned earlier: "I have always known (with absolute certainty) that I did not sing well." I feel painfully insecure in this area, even though I realize now that good singing is a learning experience. Singing, I think, is very personal. Especially when it is bad singing!

The more I ponder all of this, the more uneasy I become. And that means it is time to stop thinking about it! I suspect, however, that I would probably turn tail and run in the opposite direction from my first voice lesson except for two factors: 1) I know the experience will make a valuable contribution to our book, and 2) I'd sure like to be able to sing GOOD!

RICKY

A MUSICAL INSTRUMENT OF OUR OWN

If you are a normal, healthy person with a speaking voice, you have a singing voice.

FRANK LAFORGE

Have you ever stopped to think of your voice as a musical instrument? That's exactly what it is! The human voice qualifies as a musical instrument as much as any other musical instrument. As a matter of fact, the human voice has more flexibility and more potential for expressive communication than any other instrument. It can perform incredible feats. And the vocal instrument is the only instrument I can think of which doesn't cost a penny to purchase, doesn't need a warranty, never needs to be polished, and travels everywhere with its owner. Why, it even comes equipped with its own special case!

A musical instrument, by definition, is an instrument designed to produce *musical tones*. It must also be able to *sustain* a tone for a desired length of time, produce controllable *pitches,* have various *volume* levels, and produce a pleasant *tone quality* (one that is free from excessive and inappropriate *noise* which would detract from its musicality). The human voice can do all of the above and do them beautifully.

If you take a quick memory trip back to your high school general science class, you may remember some discussion about sound being transmitted through the air via sound waves. From the standpoint of the traditional musician, if the sound wave is regular in its pattern, the sound which is heard is called a MUSICAL TONE. If the sound wave is irregular in its pattern, it produces NOISE.

The distinction between noise and musical tone is of particular interest to the singer. A singer learns to produce musical tones first, then he interrupts the tone with various noises. In the singer's vocabulary, the tones are called VOWELS, and the noises are called CONSONANTS.

A vowel is a voiced speech sound that has no interference in the air stream by the lips, teeth, or tongue and can be sustained without change for as long as the breath continues. A consonant is a speech sound which has interference somewhere in the mouth, caused by the teeth, tongue, or lips. The consonant may be sustained or plosive, voiced or unvoiced.

When a new student begins to train his vocal instrument, he concentrates first upon producing musical tones. Therefore, he works initially on vowel sounds. After he gains sufficient control over the use of his voice so that he can clearly sustain defined vowel sounds without unnecessary muscular tension, he is ready to add consonants and inflection.

When vowels and consonants are put together in singing, they produce meaningful language. Thus, singing is an art that combines music and language . . . something that no other musical instrument can do.

Other instruments also produce noise, but since it is noise that has no communicative purpose, it only serves to detract from the beauty of the musical tone. There are a few songs that don't have words (vocalises and scat singing), but, primarily, a singer is concerned with the optimum combination of music and language. (The words of a song are referred to as the text, poem, or lyrics.)

MUSICAL TONE is composed of the same properties as the specifications of a musical instrument mentioned earlier. They are: DURATION,

PITCH, VOLUME (intensity), and TONE COLOR. All four elements are measurable and can be studied scientifically.

A person can go to a scientific laboratory, test his voice and emerge with clinical data in hand. If he wished to achieve optimum technical use of his vocal instrument, he could train and test himself until he reached a plateau of having physically perfected his musical instrument. Unfortunately, this wouldn't automatically make him an acceptable singer or performer, because the best test of whether a person is a successful singer is simply if other people want to listen to him sing! Technique is not enough, because singing also involves energy, emotion, creative interpretation, and communication.

Every musical instrument, including the vocal instrument, has three basic components that contribute to the production of a musical tone: an ACTUATOR, to supply the energy; a VIBRATOR, to give the pitch; and a RESONATOR, to provide the amplification. In stringed instruments (such as violin or guitar), for example, the bow or hand that stimulates the string is the actuator; the string is the vibrator; and the body of the instrument, which amplifies the tone of the string, is the resonator.

In the vocal instrument, the actuator is the breath or lungs, the vibrator is the vocal cords (located in the larynx), and the resonators are the air cavities above the larynx (the throat, mouth, and occasionally the nasal passages).

The specific muscles which comprise the vocal instrument are part of the interrelated muscle structure of the entire body. If the singer is overly tense in his legs, arms, shoulders, neck, face, hands, anywhere, this body tension will adversely affect his singing.

Everyone who has a healthy functioning larynx, who is without a disorder of the resonance cavities (such as a cleft palate), and who can perceive pitches well enough to hear a melody, possesses the basic instrument with which to produce beautiful sounds. BEAUTIFUL SINGING IS NOT THE PRODUCT OF A MYSTERIOUS TALENT GRANTED TO A PREFERRED FEW. INSTEAD, IT IS THE RESULT OF LEARNING TO USE SKILLFULLY THE NORMAL PHYSICAL FEATURES THAT WE ALL POSSESS.

What about people with "natural talent"? What about those lucky souls who never took a voice lesson in their lives but who open their mouths and sing like canaries? The "natural talent" is someone who accidentally happened to learn good singing habits instead of bad ones, probably by imitating a good singer (his parents, a friend, a teacher, a recording). I would suspect that these "natural talents," who are very few in number, sang a great deal when they were children and also listened to a lot of music. Sing-

THE VOCAL INSTRUMENT

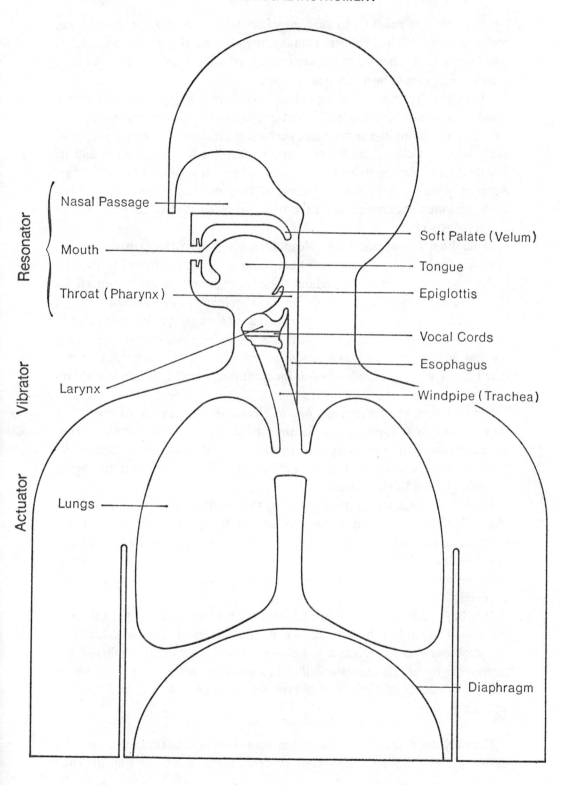

ing is much like running, in that all of us who have healthy, functioning bodies can run. With competent training and after much practice, most of us could learn to run better, faster, smoother, and with greater endurance . . . even if we happen to be a "natural" runner.

About two hundred years ago, Italy gave every appearance of being a "land of natural opera singers." What happened was that opera, which was born in Italy during the seventeenth century, flourished among the people at every level of society. The Italians were as familiar then with opera and its special style of singing as Americans are today with popular music. (Today, America gives the appearance of being a "land of natural pop singers," because pop music is around us all the time, we listen to it often, and we imitate it quite well.)

In addition to operatic arias, Neapolitan songs (the lusty, rhythmic, distinctive popular songs—such as "O Sole Mio"—which originated in the city of Naples) were sung all throughout the country, even on street corners. To sing these songs effectively, the singer was required to use wide vocal range, good dynamic control and *bel canto* singing. *Bel canto* (which translates as "beautiful singing") is a type of singing which emphasizes the voice as a musical instrument. (Singing opera arias and art songs necessitates a particular type of vocal production which incorporates flexibility in range and volume.)

Not only were the Italians exposed to a considerable amount of opera, but they listened to it carefully and learned to sing it well by *imitation*. They learned to use their voices very expansively . . . with appropriate diction and good range, dynamics, and emotional content. They sang from the heart, beautifully. Like Enrico Caruso did!

During the past ten or twenty years, the tradition of Italian music has changed. Opera is no longer the medium of the general public. With the diminishing amount of operatic singing being heard, less operatic singing is being imitated during the vitally important formative years. Consequently, Italy no longer seems to be producing as many "natural opera singers" as it once did.

It is important to realize that each of us is the owner of a superb musical instrument which has the potential for producing beautiful sounds. Learning to "play" our vocal instrument is a challenge, and meeting the challenge is a thoroughly rewarding experience that benefits the whole person . . . physically, emotionally, spiritually, and even interpersonally as a singer interacts with his audience.

Not only does each of us possess our own built-in musical instrument, but each of us uses it every single day . . . from the time we wake up until the time we go to sleep. Although no one goes around singing all the time, we do go around talking all the time. Normal speech contains the musical elements of pitch, rhythm, tempo, volume, tone color, and diction . . . all of which transfer directly into singing. Your own speech is very likely more musical than you now realize.

PITCH IN SPEECH

Everyone speaks on pitches, but since we don't usually sustain our tones while speaking, the pitches are in a constant state of flux and are heard as inflections (pitch changes). In daily speech, most people use a 1½-octave range in pitch! The normal range of pitches used in everyday speaking is sufficient to sing any song written within a 1½-octave range. Many songs, both popular and art songs, are written within this range. There are a lot of people, who speak with wider inflections, whose speaking pitch range spans 2½ octaves or more. Most operatic arias require no more than a 2½-octave range!

Inflections are gliding pitch changes. These changes may occur within one word or within a sentence. For instance, if you make the factual statement "Beverly Sills is a WONDERFUL singer!" you will probably drop the pitch of your voice on the last word ("singer"). But, if you thought Beverly Sills was the name of a city in Southern California, you would probably say: "Beverly Sills is a wonderful SINGER?" using a rising inflection at the end of the sentence.

Wide changes from our normal speech inflection patterns occur in moments of excitement ("Come on, team . . . score that touchdown!"), surprise ("You mean the party was LAST night?"), disbelief ("Doctor, did you say TRIPLETS?"), fear ("Watch out for that car; it's out of control!"), joy ("This is the happiest moment of my life!"), anger ("I most certainly DID pay my income tax in 1977!").

Pitch has a tendency to rise as the volume of speech gets louder. Mothers who call their children in for dinner use considerable volume, and usually a high pitch, in their initial call. When the kids don't come home immediately, as they usually don't, then Mother increases her volume, raises her pitch, and her shout turns into a scream. As if by magic, the kids materialize from all directions.

The way a person uses inflection is a good indicator of his basic body-energy type, his mood, emotion, social circumstance (casual or formal), regional background, ethnic background, socioeconomic background, educational background, and even the state of his inebriation!

Although almost everyone uses inflection in speech, there are a few people who do not. They are called MONOTONES. A true monotone suffers either from a hearing problem or from some type of laryngeal dysfunction. The basis of his problem may be organic (physical) or functional (behavioral). If the problem is organic, pitch reproduction will be difficult, if not impossible, unless it can be corrected medically. If the problem is functional, a speech therapist is able to provide the necessary professional advice and assistance to overcome the difficulty in pitch perception and reproduction. A speech therapist is trained to administer diagnostic tests to determine whether the problem is organic or functional and to make recommendations about possible treatment.

Many people suffer from the misapprehension that they are monotones when in fact they are not. If you "think" you are a monotone, tape record some of your spoken conversation or verbal reading. Very often when people record their voices and then listen to the playback, they are astonished to discover that they utilize a considerable amount of inflection in speech, even though they had previously "thought" they used none.

Many people do speak *monotonously,* but they are not true monotones. They are people who learned poor and boring speech habits. The droning habit can easily be changed if a reasonable effort is made to change it. A "droner" can work by himself at home with a tape recorder, or he can seek professional help from a speech teacher. He can also help himself by taking singing lessons, because singing involves the use of pitch discrimination. Whatever method the droner selects, improvement will occur if he makes consistent and repetitious effort to speak with inflection.

Some people use such a wide inflection range that their speech sounds insincere and cloying. Have you ever heard someone say: "Oh! What a darling little puppy dog. Come here poochi-ooochi-ooochi." Dreadful, isn't it? Sometimes women are guilty of using unnecessarily wide inflections in casual conversation, thus giving their speech (and themselves) less authority. A speaker can achieve a secure, adult conversational tone by using a considerably smaller inflection range while maintaining interesting expression and variety, or by using a medium amount of inflection that is appropriate for emphasis and clarity. Too narrow a use of inflection results in dullness and the droning problem that we mentioned earlier.

Some people alter their natural pitch in order to achieve a stronger sense of sex identification. Men tend to be the worst offenders here and will frequently choose a low speaking pitch because they believe it to be "more masculine." If they select a pitch that is too low for their natural range, the unfortunate result is that the quality of their speech is strained and unpleasant to their listeners. Some men speak in a higher pitch than is indicated by the natural pitch range of their voice. When this happens, their voice quality seems unsubstantial and weak. Speaking in the "wrong" pitch range is not limited to men. Women sometimes make the same mistake.

If you have access to a piano or some other pitch-producing instrument, you can discover the best speaking range for you. Begin by singing from an easy, comfortable pitch down to as low a pitch as possible. Check what pitch this is on the piano. Then sing up as high as you can (without being concerned about the quality). Men should use falsetto and women their high flute-like tones. Again check the pitch on the piano. Then count the number of half steps (black and white keys) between your two extreme pitches (the highest and lowest you can go). Divide by four (4) to discover the twenty-fifth percentile. That note will be your OPTIMUM SPEAKING PITCH, a good average speaking pitch for you in normal conversation. It should be the median pitch of your speech, the pitch to which you return "home" after embellishing it with appropriate inflection changes.

To discover what median pitch you are presently using (your MODAL PITCH), tape-record your speaking voice while using your usual conversational tone. Check (on the piano) the pitches that you use most often. You may have to experiment a bit on the piano to locate the pitches because in speech we don't sustain our pitches. They are constantly in flux, even within one word. Keep on trying, though, and when you do locate your modal pitch, compare it (the one you presently use) with the optimum pitch discovered above (the one you should use). Are they roughly the same, or did you find a wide variation between them? A wide variation (four or more half steps) would indicate that you should concentrate on either raising or lowering the general pitch level of your speaking voice in order to more closely approximate what is natural for you.

Most people are surprised to discover just how high a sound they can make. Are you a good actor? If so, record the sounds you would make if you called out the window to your neighbor's house. Then scream as if you were at a football game and the home team just scored the winning touchdown. Let the pitch go up! Scream high and check the pitch on the piano. I predict you will be surprised at how high it is.

Very often the person who believes most strongly that he "can't carry a tune" will be the first to change his mind when he listens to a tape recording of his speaking voice. He will simply be astounded at the variety of inflection he uses in everyday speech. When he hears how "musical" his speech actually is, it becomes a lot more believable that with practice he should be able to sustain these pitches in singing.

RHYTHM AND TEMPO IN SPEECH

Rhythm and tempo, two of the most basic elements of singing, are also primary elements of speech. Tempo refers to the rate (how fast or how slowly) at which we speak. It is surprising how many people have little or no idea of how fast they speak. Do you? Record yourself and see!

The following exercise will help you discover your normal reading tempo. How does it compare to your normal conversational tempo? (Conversational rate is usually about seven or eight words per minute slower than reading tempo.)

> Choose several paragraphs in a book or article. Read the words aloud and note how far you read in one minute's time. One hundred and sixty words per minute is an easily comprehended rate for the average type of material (151 to 181 words per minute are considered satisfactory reading tempos). Technical material should be read more slowly for comprehension by the listener. Very easy material can be read faster, even up to 190 words per minute. If you read any faster than that, you will lose your audience. The faster you read, the better you must articulate in order to be understood.

Everyone's speech has a characteristic rhythm that is defined by the unique grouping of his words. The groupings will fall into repetitive patterns. This is what enables us to define a person's speech into the various classifications listed in the Energy Release Chart on page 30. A person's general speech rhythm (whether it is smooth, jerky, clipped, has long or short pauses, drawl, etc.) remains distinctively his whether he speaks slowly or fast or whether he is happy or sad, angry or calm. It is difficult to disguise our natural speech rhythm. Tempo, on the other hand, can be changed easily.

VOLUME IN SPEECH

In speech, the primary consideration about volume is simply whether we speak loudly enough to be heard but not so loudly as to be offensive. The volume of both speech and singing relates to the loudness of our vowel sounds, *not* the consonants. Consonants are strictly limited in the amount of volume with which they can be produced.

A person may be in the habit of speaking so loudly that we label him a "shouter," but we won't be able to understand him (to know what he is saying) if he doesn't articulate his consonants. We will just hear loud, slurred, unintelligible sounds. On the other hand, a person can speak at a low volume level and be clearly understood if he articulates distinctly.

Volume combines with inflection and rhythm to lend contour, emphasis, and greater meaning to what is being said. Notice how the meaning changes in the following sentence when you alter the volume level of various words (say the capitalized words more loudly):

"She is a VERY good student."   (implying excellence)
"She is a very GOOD student."   (in contrast to being a bad one)
"She is a very good STUDENT."   (but not a professional)
"SHE is a very good student."   (but the boy is not)

TONE COLOR IN SPEECH

Tone color refers to the distinctive quality of sound that characterizes every person's voice—whether it is mellow, shrill, harsh, soft, rough, nasal, smooth, muted, etc. The qualities can vary according to mood, volume, emotion, and what is being said.

Tone color is an element of speech over which the speaker can exercise considerable control. When he employs undesirable qualities, he should exercise a lot of control and change them! The tone color of our voice has an enormous effect upon the people around us . . . so much so that it may determine whether others are receptive to listening to what we have to say. In Chapter Four there is a lengthy discussion on tone color and how to create new vocal qualities.

DICTION IN SPEECH

Diction refers to the manner of the articulation of individual speech sounds (consonants and vowels) and to the way we pronounce words. Like tone color, we can, and sometimes should, exercise control over our diction.

Each of us has ethnic and regional backgrounds that influence our pronunciation. Usually we needn't be too concerned about these types of accents unless they result in pronunciation that is considered substandard and therefore less acceptable. People in the public eye—business leaders, politicians, performers—often find it advantageous to cultivate pronunciation which is considered standard over a wide geographical area simply because it is more generally acceptable. Actors must have a considerable amount of flexibility with diction so that they can portray different characterizations convincingly.

STANDARD PRONUNCIATION is the way in which the educated people of a region pronounce their words in a cultivated, acceptable fashion.
SUBSTANDARD PRONUNCIATION tends to be lazy or sloppy speech
with mispronunciations and colloquialisms. With a little study and a lot of
practice we can pronounce the English language any way we desire. If Eliza
Doolittle in *My Fair Lady* can change, so can we!

Singing requires a clear understanding and good use of appropriate diction. "Old Man River" and "I'm (Jist) a Girl Who (Cain't) Say No" would
sound ridiculous if sung with a Harvard accent.

In the beginning of my professional career I performed the role of Hansel
(in the opera *Hansel and Gretel* by Humperdinck) for an audience of children at a theater in upstate New York. My regional background is southern,
from Louisiana, and at the point in the opera, when Hansel steals a cookie
from the witch's house, he turns to Gretel and sings: "This cookie I will
share." However, my southern version sounded like: "This cookie Ah will
Shay-uh." The house convulsed in laughter and I resolved that that would be
the last time my southern heritage showed up inappropriately in my singing.
Red of face and filled with chagrin, I went home and worked on my operatic
diction until it no longer revealed any trace of southern heritage.

EXERCISE 1

PURPOSE: To determine the reality of your existing speech habits.

To determine the reality of your existing speech habits—in the areas of
pitch, volume, inflection, tempo, rhythm, tone color, and diction—record
yourself on tape. We hear our voice through our inner ears, and this perception is different from what we hear through our outer ears. Don't be surprised if your recorded voice sounds considerably different to you. It's the
REAL you! It's how other people hear you.

Record yourself while reading some material from a book. Then record
yourself participating in spontaneous conversation. A lively party is a good
time to make such a recording, because you can forget that the recorder is
on and your conversation will be more spontaneous and natural. Your
friends might also enjoy hearing their voices on tape!

Listen carefully to the two different tapes and then answer the following
questions:

1. Are the pitches, rhythms, tempos, tone colors, and diction similar or
   different in the two tapes?

2. What is your diction like? Heavy regional accent? Well-articulated? Easily understood? Mispronunciations? Would you hire this person (you) to work as a salesman, or executive, or someone who would meet the public?

3. On what pitches do you speak? Is the median pitch suitable for your range?

4. What type of rhythm do you use? Short sentences, long sentences? Do you speak in a slow and sustained "laid back" fashion? Do you speak in spurts? Are your pauses long or short?

5. What is the tempo of your speech? Is it always the same or are there variations?

6. Does the pitch of your voice vary with appropriate inflections, or does it remain monotonous and droning?

7. What is the volume level of your speech? Do you speak louder or softer than your friends? Do you use an appropriate volume level for the occasion and the subject matter?

8. When you speak louder, do you also speak higher?

9. What tonal qualities do you use in speech (twangy, mellow, thin, rich, raspy, etc.)?

10. How do you interrelate in speech flow with others? Do you cut people off when they are speaking? Do you respond in a smooth, rhythmical flow?

11. How do you go about developing ideas, giving instructions, telling stories? Are they stated clearly and logically?

12. What is the emotional tone of your speech? Does it accurately reflect your real emotion? Is the tone aggressive even when you wish it to be gentle? Is the tone supplicating even when you are feeling justifiable anger? Do you use baby talk?

13. Can you define the way you release energy in your speech by using the categories listed in the Energy Chart on page 30?

It will take some time and thought to answer all of these questions, but it is a worthwhile effort. Not only will it give you more insight into the reality of your own speaking habits, but it should crystallize the fact that YOUR SPEECH ALREADY CONTAINS THE BASIC ELEMENTS OF SINGING. Compared to speech, singing is simply a more highly defined, refined, and amplified usage of pitch, rhythm, tempo, volume, tone color, and diction.

EXERCISE 2

PURPOSE: To read a poem to music and reflect the energy of the music in
        the spoken word.

1. Choose a poem.

   This can be any poem, or poetic prose, or text from a song. Be sure it
   expresses ideas that have meaning for you.

2. Choose a recorded piece of music.

   Pick out some instrumental music without any singing. Singing would interfere with the vocal line you are going to make in speech. The energy or
   emotion of the music should relate to the energy and emotion of the
   words.

3. Familiarize yourself with both the words and music.

4. Read the words as the music plays, trying to capture and express the energy
   and emotion of the music in your reading.

CHAPTER FOUR

FROM SPEECH TO MUSIC AND SONG

———————— ✳ ✳ ✳ ————————

"AFTER THE FIRST LESSON"

My first singing lesson is over! It's history . . . and I "lived" to tell the tale. I feel somewhat like a soldier who has survived his first battle. Not only did I manage to emerge unscathed, but I learned a few things in the process.

After the lesson was over, Joan said that early in the lesson (while I was taking a series of deep breaths, as instructed), she thought I might faint. At that exact point in time, I had strongly entertained the same possibility. Big, strong, brave me, who never fainted before in my life, came close to keeling over!

That's an accurate indication of the state of mind that preceded the lesson, continuing till the session was about half over. As the lesson time drew near, I began to tremble. Then the moment of truth was at hand. My mouth was parched. I had to drink a glass of water. Then another.

I finally began to relax as the lesson progressed, primarily because Joan was very supportive. She never asked me to do something that I couldn't do, or didn't feel capable of trying.

The lesson consisted of listening to and then reproducing the vowel sound "Ah" while making high, soft, bell-like sounds and low, loud, firm sounds. The entire lesson seemed more related to speaking than to singing. But then I remembered what Joan had told me earlier—that singing is an extension of speech and that singing is sustained speech.

Especially during the early part of the lesson, I found it very uncomfortable to make any sound whatsoever while looking directly at the teacher. It was considerably easier to gaze out the window to Joan's right, at the bookcase to her immediate left, above her head, or at the piano keyboard. Anywhere but at her face. After a while, I needed to look at her mouth to watch how she used it in demonstration. But I never felt comfortable enough to look at her eyes for any length of time. The temptation to giggle insanely was too great.

We worked for a while in front of a mirrored wall, where it was even harder to meet my own eyes than it had been to meet Joan's! Surprisingly, when I did my first practice session alone at home this morning, the mirror seemed friendlier. It would have been difficult, if not impossible, to practice successfully without the aid of the mirror.

By the time the thirty-minute lesson was finished, I felt as if the little black cloud that had been hovering over my anxious head for days had suddenly vanished. I felt free as a bird. Later, in the privacy of my bathroom, I warbled like one too.

At the conclusion of the lesson, Joan told me that I have a three-octave range. Singing most songs, she said, requires a range of about one-and-a-half octaves. I have an entire octave to spare. How about that! She also explained that we would continue to work on vowels, pitches, and dynamic levels for another three or four lessons before attempting to sing a song. Hooray . . . I have been reprieved for three or four more weeks!

RICKY

FROM SPEECH TO SINGING

In the last chapter we discussed the many similarities between speech and singing and the fact that in speech we are already using many of the elements found in singing. If singing is so closely related to speech, what, then, is the difference between them? The difference is MUSIC. Speech becomes singing when the voice is used to make music. The primary purpose of speech is to communicate. The primary purpose of singing is to make a creative emotional expression in music.

Sometimes drawing the line between speech and singing is difficult to do because there is a gray area between them. Some speech is extremely close to being musical and some singing is very close to being speech. Usually, though, speech becomes singing when the vocal sounds are used to create music . . . when the sounds are sustained and structured in a rhythmical order, usually in a melody with implied harmonic structure.

In general, music is sound that is put together in a balanced organization which is energized and structured by rhythm. Music contains the elements of pitch (melody), tone color, rhythm, dynamics, form, and harmony. All these elements are put together purposely to create a personal expression or an emotional impact.

Music does not need words to achieve impact, but in song we have the ultimate—musical impact and words (language) that combine together to create a new dimension for emotional expression. In listening to different songs you will notice that some songs emphasize words more than music, others emphasize music more than words, and in other songs they are balanced.

Each of us has a vocal instrument that we use every day in speech. With the addition of music, our vocal instrument becomes a musical instrument that each of us can learn to use as effectively as we desire in the production of song. Since singing is the product of our musical instrument and song is the music produced by it, let's delve more deeply into the basic elements of music and song. An increased understanding and awareness of these musical elements will help us to make the transition from speech to singing. Once again, these musical elements are:

1. PITCH
2. TONE COLOR
3. RHYTHM
4. DYNAMICS
5. HARMONY
6. FORM

CARRYING A TUNE

Melodies (tunes) are made up of individual pitches in a rhythmical order, which are put together in such a fashion that they usually imply harmony and make orderly sense to our musical ear.

An appealing melody has a sense of direction, a sense of "pull" from one note to another. It seems as if each subsequent note is predestined, as if no other note could take its place . . . a sense of "rightness" prevails. For the listener, this rightness induces feelings of deep satisfaction, vitality, and sometimes even of power. In an inspired melody there is a sense of energy which is found not only in songs having vigorous rhythm, but also in melodies which are gentle or have long lyrical lines.

In order to sing a melody, the singer must have two basic abilities. They are:

1. PITCH PERCEPTION and PITCH MEMORY (mental images)
2. PITCH REPRODUCTION (vocal sound)

Once a pitch is sounded, the singer must mentally perceive that exact pitch, remember it and then reproduce it through an automatic neuromotor action in the larynx (voice box). Since most people are blessed with normal hearing and normal larynges, learning to sing a melody, then, becomes essentially:

1. Learning to LISTEN more efficiently, and
2. Learning to USE the LARYNX more efficiently.

If you were able to perform the Chapter One exercises, including singing "Row Your Boat," then you possess the two basic abilities required to sing a melody. If you encountered some difficulty with the exercises, you probably still have the two abilities but in an undeveloped state. You will improve with practice.

If, however, you experienced major difficulty in performing the exercises and if in the past you have been aware of persistent problems in matching pitch or singing a melody ("carrying a tune"), there are some suggestions at the end of this section which should help you to evaluate and remedy your situation.

Pitch in Music

According to Webster's *New World Dictionary,* PITCH is "the highness or lowness of a sound due to vibrations of sound waves." The faster the vibration, the higher the sound; the slower the vibration, the lower the sound. In the voice, pitch is produced by the action of the vocal cords . . . specifically, a particular pitch is determined by the number of times the vocal cords open and close per second.

How Pitch Is Produced

The vocal cords consist of two horizontal bands of extremely flexible muscles, each band being about ¾-inch long, which are attached to ligaments and cartilages in the larynx (the Adam's apple). The vocal cords are joined together in the front and open in the back when they are in a relaxed state. When they are being used, they are closed both in the front and in the back.

When we make a sound, two cartilages in the back of the larynx move together, bringing the vocal bands/cords together. You can experience this phenomenon by taking a breath and pretending that you are about to lift a heavy weight. You will feel the closure of the vocal cords in the throat. The closure occurs to prevent the escape of air—therefore, giving you extra power to lift the weight.

If you could look down into your windpipe—as a doctor does when he uses a small mirror to examine your throat—you would see the vocal cords: two bands of muscles running parallel to each other, located in the larynx, which is in the windpipe (trachea). The larynx, sometimes called the "voice box," is made of cartilage. Located just underneath the chin, it is what's popularly called the Adam's apple and, Women's Lib notwithstanding, the larynx is somewhat smaller in women. A man's vocal cords, in their relaxed state, are longer and thicker than those of a woman. Their greater mass accounts for men's voices being lower-pitched.

In addition to producing pitch, the vocal cords act as a valve which, when closed, prevents air from escaping from the lungs and also assists in preventing foreign matter from entering the lungs. When the air pressure from the lungs exceeds the strength of the gently closed valve (vocal cords), the vocal cords give way, opening for a tiny fraction of a second and allowing some of the air to escape. Almost immediately, the vocal cords spring back together because of their muscular and elastic nature and also because of aerodynamic factors. The following diagram illustrates the positions of the open and closed vocal cords when viewed in a doctor's small mirror. The area labeled "Front" is the Adam's apple.

OPEN AND CLOSED VOCAL CORDS

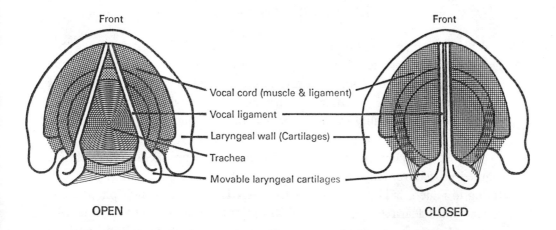

Vocal cord (muscle & ligament)

Vocal ligament

Laryngeal wall (Cartilages)

Trachea

Movable laryngeal cartilages

OPEN   CLOSED

In the production of any sound, including speech and singing, there is a balance between the amount of tension in the vocal cords and in the amount of breath pressure. As the breath pressure increases, overriding the tension in the larynx, the vocal cords separate briefly and a puff of air escapes. The vocal cords quickly snap back into place, and then open immediately to permit yet another puff of air to escape. This opening-and-closing action occurs incredibly quickly and repeatedly. If it occurs 440 times in one second, the pitch of *A* above middle *C* is produced. This is the pitch to which an orchestra tunes.

The entire opening and closing procedure occurs so quickly that we call it a vibration. It is similar to the way a person can make his lips flap by blowing air through them. When the tension in the lips is increased, the lips will vibrate—opening and closing very quickly. A good trumpet player can actually play a tune with his lips by skillfully varying tension and breath pressure.

Pitch is produced by the number of vibrations per second, with the faster vibrations producing the higher pitches. Each octave on the piano is mathematically related to the next. *A* above middle *C* is produced by 440 puffs (vibrations) per second (called HERTZ). One octave lower, the *A* is produced by 220 hertz, and an octave below that, it is produced by 110 hertz.

In singing, control of pitch depends upon a delicate balance between the breath pressure and the tension of the muscles inside the voice box. However, the actions of the vocal cords and voice box are not controlled directly by the singer. They are governed by mental concept and auditory memory of pitch and through growing awareness and kinesthetic memory in the vocal instrument.

PITCH PROBLEMS

When someone says, "I can't sing," what he usually means is either that he can't "carry a tune" (stay on pitch) or that he doesn't like the sound (quality) of his singing voice. In this section we will deal with the problems encountered in carrying a tune and in finding and staying on a melody. We will discuss voice quality in the latter part of this chapter, in the section on tone color.

First, let us repeat that for a normal person the reproduction of pitch is a learned procedure. Anyone who can sing within three notes of the one he is trying to match, is NOT tone-deaf. He CAN LEARN to match pitches. Everyone must learn to reproduce pitch, except those very few people who seem to have a keen awareness of pitch from their early years, and an even smaller number of people who have what is called "perfect pitch." (People with perfect pitch can reproduce an accurate pitch completely from memory, without any reference to other pitches. If we were in the middle of a forest and we asked them to sing an *A* [440 hertz], they could do it!) Incidentally, folk singer Pete Seeger reports that scientists discovered recently that horses have perfect pitch!*

Perfect pitch is not a learned skill. The few people, and all the horses,

* *Henscratches and Flyspecks* (New York: Berkley Publishing Corporation, 1973) p. 21.

who possess the ability were born with it. Everyone else, including most professional musicians, has to learn pitch perception and pitch reproduction. And what we learn is *relative* pitch relationships—whether one pitch is higher or lower than another, and how much higher or lower it is.

We learn to match pitch the same way we learned to throw a basketball through a hoop. We watched someone sink a shot, we imitated their motions and then we practiced, practiced, practiced. It's unlikely that we sank the ball on our first try, so we kept on trying until we scored more "hits" than "misses." The same holds true for "hitting" pitch accurately. We need to find a good model-singer, we need to know how to listen to our model, we need to imitate him or her, and we need to sing a great deal. Then we will improve.

Since the reproduction of pitch first requires discriminating pitch perception, let's consider the way you listen now and how your listening might be improved. Check out the status of your listening by answering the following questions:

Listening

—— A. I can sing a low note and then a higher note, and perceive a difference in relative highness and lowness of pitch.

—— B. I can think of a familiar song, such as "Home on the Range," and mentally "hear" the melody in my imagination.

—— C. I can listen to two people singing together, particularly when they sing without accompaniment, and usually know if they are singing the same pitches or different pitches in harmony.

—— D. I can hear a short melody played once on the piano, and then repeated, and know if it is the same melody.

—— E. I can recognize the melody of a familiar song such as "The Star-spangled Banner" when it is played by instruments and there are no words. I recognize it because of the melody and not because of other cues like rhythm or the fact that everyone is standing with their hands over their hearts.

—— F. I can hear two notes played successively, a third apart, on the piano and perceive the difference between them. (A third would be the distance between three white keys, i.e., from C_4 to E_4.)

If you can determine the above, then your listening problems are not due to organic disturbances. You will be able to improve by doing some exercises. If you cannot do any of the above, you may have a hearing or perception problem. Our suggestion would be to visit a speech-therapy clinic and request that a therapist test your hearing. Very often there is a solution.

Improve Your Listening

The following are elementary exercises in ear training which will help you learn to listen more attentively:

1. Using a piano (or other pitch-producing instrument), strike one note and then another and determine whether you can hear the difference.
2. Sing a pitch and try to find it on the piano.
3. Have a friend play or sing two notes successively.
   Do you hear a difference? If you are using a piano, start with notes that are three white keys apart, and end by reducing the distance to two notes that adjoin one another.
4. Have a friend play or sing a three- or four-note melody, then have them do it again, changing one note. Do you hear the difference?

Where Am I?

(LISTENING AND PITCH REPRODUCTION)

Indicate (with a √) the status of your present abilities in listening and pitch reproduction.

—— a. I can perceive pitch, but I can NEVER seem to sing the pitch I am perceiving.

—— b. I can whistle pitches and melodies, but I can't sing them.

—— c. Sometimes I can match pitch, but I'm not sure when it is correct. Someone else must confirm it for me.

—— d. I can match some pitches sometimes, and I usually know if I'm doing it right or wrong.

—— e. I can match some pitches, but not enough to sing a recognizable melody, even with someone singing or playing along with me at all times.

—— f. I can sing "Row Your Boat" well enough for someone to recognize the song, even if they hear me sing it without words (humming or substituting "la" for the words).

—— g. Sometimes I can sing a melody well, but other times I can't seem to do it at all, even when it is the same melody. Sometimes I can "hear" it in my mind and sometimes I can't.

—— h. Sometimes I can sing the melody just fine, but if I once get off, I can't seem to get back on.

—— i. I can hear and sing melody IF other singers or instruments are assisting me with a strong melody line. If they perform the harmony only and leave me alone with the melody, I get lost.

If you checked categories "a" or "b," a laryngeal disorder may or may not be indicated. It might be wise to have a professional check-up performed by a speech therapist or otolaryngologist. If you fit in categories "b" through "i," it indicates that you have minor problems with pitch perception and reproduction resulting from inept learning experiences. Such learning shortcomings can be improved through ear and voice training. The "help yourself" suggestions listed below are effective and can easily be performed in your own home.

No one hears himself (through his inner ear) the way others hear him. Since it is important to hear how you really sound, tape-record your singing voice. If you don't have access to a recorder, then try to get some feedback about your singing voice from another person. We hope you can record your voice, because most people can more readily hear and determine the accuracy of their own pitch reproduction when they listen to their recorded voice.

Ear Training and Improving Pitch Reproduction

a. Repeat the elementary exercises for ear training on page 54.

b. Use a cassette player to record your singing responses to the playing of a single note on the piano. Can you hear whether you matched the pitch? It is easier to perceive your recorded pitches than those done "live."

c. Ask a friend to sing the melody and you sing along. Pick a friend of the same sex so that you will both sing the same pitches. It is sometimes easier to match pitches when singing along with another person than when singing with the piano.

d. Sing along with a recording of a familiar song that has a strong melody and see whether you can stay with the tune.

e. Play a melody on the piano and sing along.

f. Play a melody and then sing it without continued support from the piano. Begin with short melodies, or portions of a melody (perhaps just three or four notes in length). Then progress to longer phrases.

If you continue to have trouble remembering a melody, keep on trying. It takes patience. If you're an impatient sort, you might consider seeking professional help from a voice teacher.

If you find that you can hear the melody in your imagination but can't seem to reproduce it vocally, again . . . just keep on trying. Yours is not a physical problem, but a learning shortcoming. Success can be yours with continued singing. Remember not to be critical of your vocal quality. Vocal muscles need time to respond. If your basic tendency is to sing quite loudly, try singing more softly and vice versa.

Long-time voice students and professional musicians develop a keen sense of pitch as a result of very attentive listening and concentrated practice. They often speak of the need for good INTONATION. Good intonation carries the matching of pitch one step further. It is the reproduction of extremely accurate and well-tuned pitch and is developed through doing a lot of careful practice (singing, singing, singing!).

TONE COLOR

When someone says he doesn't like the sound of his singing, what he is referring to is the TONE COLOR of his voice, the QUALITY of his voice. Usually he believes that he is "stuck" with his singing quality till Doomsday. But he is mistaken. He can change the tone color of his singing just as he changes it every day in his speech.

Each of the many language sounds of the human voice can be produced in a variety of ways. Vocal sounds can be mellow, nasal, smooth, rough, beautiful, ugly, clear, harsh, hoarse, breathy, pleasant, strident, sweet, throaty, aggressive, light, strong, rich, deep, etc.—all of which are different tone colors, different tone qualities. When we cry, whine, sob, grunt, shout, scream, etc., we change the tone color of our voice.

We change tone color without even being conscious of doing so. We do it because—depending upon what we wish to say—we communicate more effectively when we change the tone of our voice. Singers who believe that they are limited to making only one singing sound should realize that they already use a wide variety of tone qualities in daily speech and that they can transfer their repertoire of speech qualities into singing.

CREATING NEW QUALITIES

One way to create new qualities in our singing voice is to change one or more elements of the music. By experimenting with the first line of the song

"The Caissons Go Rolling Along," as directed in this next exercise, you can experience changes in tone color.

The Caissons Go Rolling Along
by: Brig. Gen. Edmund L. Gruber

O - ver   hill,   o - ver   dale, We have

hit the dust - y trail, And those cais-sons go roll - ing a - long.

First, sing the line in a rousing march tempo. Sing it briskly, vigorously, giving special emphasis to each of the capitalized words.

"Over HILL, over DALE, We have HIT the dusty TRAIL,"

Second, CHANGE THE VOLUME of the line, making it considerably softer.

"Over HILL, over DALE, We have HIT the dusty TRAIL,"

Is there a change in vocal quality? You may notice a small change, depending upon how significantly you altered the volume. You may or may not like the difference, but that isn't the point of this exercise. Right now you just want to experiment with sound. If, in the process, you find a quality that pleases you . . . great! If not, then just enjoy exploring the different ways of sound-making.

Third, CHANGE THE PITCH, using any volume you wish. Sing higher or lower than you did before.

"Over HILL, over DALE, We have HIT the dusty TRAIL,"

Then change the volume again. Do you hear any color changes?

Fourth, CHANGE THE WAY YOU USE THE WORDS. This song lends itself to a percussive reading, to punching and clipping the words, giving considerable emphasis to consonants and singing very short vowels (i.e., stressing the consonants in order to gain percussiveness for the march feeling). Try singing the line with longer vowels—that is, actually making the vowels last longer. The words will be less clipped. Keep your original quick tempo, but think of the melody as sustained instead of percussive. If you think "sustained," you will add intensity to the vowels and consequently to the vocal line.

"Over HILL, over DALE, We have HIT the dusty TRAIL,"

Did the vowel sounds have intensity, vibrancy, energy? This is your goal, so if the vowels were listless or passive, try to energize them. Also keep the consonants crisp and clear.

Fifth, CHANGE THE EMOTION. Since this is only an exercise, it doesn't matter whether the emotion fits the song. A change in attitude often produces the most distinct change in tone color. Change your attitude from aggressive to calm, from happy to sad, from confident to insecure.

"Over hill, over dale, We have hit the dusty trail,"

Remember that you can expand your repertoire of singing tone colors through imagination, imitation, and experimentation. If you feel adventurous, try the next exercise in which you will accomplish changes in tone color by changing your emotion.

Sing the line—"Over hill, over dale, We have hit the dusty trail"—in the following ways.

1. Sing the words while thinking of yourself as a U. S. Army Master Sergeant barking out orders to his new recruits. Make the sounds brusque, abrupt, a cross between speech and singing. Maintain rhythm and melody even though you are as close to speech as to singing.
2. Sing the line as if they were the words of the most romantic love song ever written. Be warm, loving, tender.
3. Sing the words while thinking of yourself as Buck Owens, popular country and western star. Pretend you are strumming a guitar accompaniment.
4. Sing the line with the feeling of joy and happiness expressed by Julie Andrews in the opening scene of the film *Sound of Music,* as she stood on a mountaintop with her arms outstretched, embracing the world and singing across the valleys.

As you sang the song in the four different ways, did you experience various vocal qualities? Did any of them please you? If not, experiment some more. If they did, remember how you got them . . . through imagination, imitation, and experimentation.

Trying to explain the quality of sound through the medium of writing is as difficult as trying to explain color to a blind man. To best understand color, one must see it; to best understand sound, one must hear it. Therefore, when we write about the qualities of sound, we must urge you to draw heavily upon your imagination . . . to "hear" in your mind various qualities which you might call "rich, smooth, rough, ugly," etc. And then we ask you to create different qualities of sound by experimenting aloud while altering musical elements and changing your own emotions. A third way to experience changes in tone color is to listen attentively to the speech and singing of others, trying to identify their different qualities of sound and then imitating the ones you like.

Tone color in our voice is determined by the use of our vocal instrument and by certain physical boundaries. The "use" of the vocal instrument refers to the manner in which we balance breath pressure with the adjustment of our vibrator (vocal cords), and to the way we shape our resonators (throat, mouth, and occasionally the nasal passages). The "boundaries" which contribute to the determination of tone color are: *sex* (whether we are male or female), *tessitura* (the four or five notes we sing most easily), *range* (how high or low we can sing), *power* (the degree of loudness that we can utilize most naturally and easily), and the *physical structure* of our face and resonating cavities.

The physical boundaries of the vocal instrument have enabled singers to classify their voices into groupings (soprano, mezzo-soprano, alto, tenor, baritone, and bass) which are determined primarily by tessitura, range, tone color, and power. The value of such a classification is that it facilitates communication, is quite useful helping us to choose music that we are able to sing most effectively, and allows composers to write more knowledgeably for the voice.

There is an acoustic phenomenon called RESONANCE that plays a significant role in determining tone color. According to the dictionary, resonance is the "amplification, intensification and modification of sound." The major way to change tone quality is to change the shape of our resonators. Since we sing on vowels, the amount of resonance in singing depends upon the way we enunciate vowels. Understanding the relationship of pitch, intensity, and the ENUNCIATION OF VOWELS is one of the most basic concepts in developing ease, control, and power in singing.

A singer can alter the shape of his soft-walled resonating cavity by changing the position of his lips, tongue, jaw, soft palate, and larynx. Different positions create varying degrees of pitch amplification. We "resonate" every time we speak or sing, and with practice, we can learn to achieve more resonance or less resonance (more amplification or less amplification).

In addition to the adjustments that occur in the resonator, the vocal cords make two significant adjustments that affect tone color. The first is the degree to which the vocal cords come together in the production of sound (voicing), and the second is the condition of the vocal cords—how thick, tense, and long they are (registration). Although these two processes occur automatically and incredibly quickly, singers can acquire considerable control through voice training and practice.

When the vocal cords do not come together at all, we whisper; when some space is left between them, we have varying degrees of breathiness in speech and singing; and when the cords come together firmly during the vibratory cycle, we have a fully voiced, efficient tone. Developing a clean, efficient, unconstricted, fully voiced tone is the basis for a good vocal technique.

REGISTRATION refers to the muscular adjustment in which the vocal cords become thicker or thinner, longer or shorter, tenser or laxer, in response to pitch and volume. It refers to a particular mode of vocal cord adjustment that produces a specific quality of sound and which differs from another adjustment which produces a different tone color. These adjustments of the vocal cords are controlled primarily by a skillful use of volume on specific pitches.

When we sing high pitches softly, a laryngeal adjustment called LIGHT REGISTRATION occurs, producing a soft, fragile quality which men recognize in their voices as falsetto. In women, the sound is clear and bell-like. When we sing low pitches loudly, an adjustment called HEAVY REGISTRATION occurs, producing a loud, firm quality. Men usually speak in this register, as do many women who have low-pitched speaking voices.

Each of us has a pitch area in our voice (called the *PASSAGIO,* meaning "passage" or "transition") which requires an especially subtle balance in muscle antagonism. One of the major aims of voice training is to develop a vocal production that is smooth from top to bottom pitch and which can negotiate all levels of dynamics and varying tone colors without any "breaks" in the voice. Aurally and physically this would result in what is called a fully blended vocal production.

In producing varying vocal qualities, beginning singers will find it significant to be aware of voicing, registration, and resonance. When a singer develops control over these three elements, he begins to discover his true voice. We will have found our "true voice" when we have sufficient vocal technique to utilize our full range (probably about three octaves) and to achieve reasonable vocal control and power (including a functional use of laryngeal adjustments and resonance); and when we sing without interfering obstacles (physical or emotional).

Discovering our true voice is a process which usually requires voice training. Even if we cannot discover it on our own, we can sing and we can change tone color in our singing. We will simply be limited in the range and scope of our singing, and therefore must sing songs that fit our present abilities.

Even though you may not like the way your voice sounds now, don't depreciate it . . . add new qualities instead. Remember too that every tonal quality has interest and value when it is used artistically and appropriately. If your voice is small (soft in volume), there are many folk songs, ballads, and lyrical operatic arias that await the sweetness of your expression. If your voice is loud and aggressive, you can sing very effectively the many songs that require exhilaration and power. One type of song fits the qualities of an Ethel Merman while a very different type of song is "right" for Olivia Newton-John. Find a song that fits you!

It is within your capability to change the quality of your voice—to make it sweeter, more powerful, more beautiful, more mellow, more ringing, more expressive. What you cannot do is to have the power of a dramatic baritone if you are a lyric tenor, nor can you sound like a coloratura soprano if you are an alto. Find the qualities that fit you!

If you continue to dislike your singing tone, and if you don't discover other, more pleasing sounds through experimentation, then you might consider seeking professional guidance from a voice teacher. However, if you continue to experiment with your voice and listen attentively to singers whose tone colors you would like to emulate and then imitate them, you should succeed in changing your voice quality. In addition, there are exercises on vowel formation (in Chapter Eight) which give suggestions to help you better understand the singing voice and its ability to vary tonal qualities.

THE SCIENTIFIC MEASUREMENT OF TONE COLOR

Sound

Tone color refers to the quality of a sound. But what exactly is a sound?

Sound is that which is perceived when the auditory nerves are stimulated by vibrations carried in the air. For example, when a guitar string is plucked, the string vibrates rapidly, thus setting the surrounding air into motion. A chain reaction occurs in which the activated particles of air interact with other particles of air to such a degree that our eardrums are stimulated and we perceive a nervous disturbance in the air called "sound."

Vibration is not just an abstract scientific theory. The physical phenomenon of vibration is so tangible that when a loud explosion occurs, the powerful vibrations in the air can break windowpanes many miles away; excessively strong sound waves can cause eardrums to rupture; singers with great vocal power can shatter drinking glasses with the strong vibrations of their voices.

When the vibrations that produce sound are regular and even, the perceived sound has a distinct pitch. A particular pitch is produced by a specific number of vibrations per second. An orchestra tunes to the pitch of "Concert A," which is 440 vibrations per second. (Remember that the term hertz substitutes for the phrase "vibrations per second," thus, Concert *A* is 440 hertz.)

Sounds are composed of waves of vibrations in the air (called sound waves). A COMPOUND sound wave derives its name from the fact that it contains multiple parts, with each part having a particular pitch. PARTIALS and OVERTONES are other terms used to refer to the multiple pitches (parts) of a compound wave. The quality (tone color) of a sound is determined by the number, intensity, and relationship of the partials within the compound wave.

In rare instances, there is a single, simple wave form composed of only one partial. A tuning fork, for example, was invented for the express purpose of producing only the first partial (also called the FUNDAMENTAL PITCH). Almost every other sound is composed of compound parts, a multiplicity of pitches which are the upper partials. When these upper partials exist in a systematic, mathematical order in relationship to the first partial, they are said to be HARMONIC PARTIALS. When the partials exist in a random way, without fitting into a systematic mathematical order, they are called INHARMONIC PARTIALS. The mathematical order of harmonic partials, which is a natural happenstance and not a man-made system, is illustrated in the following diagram.

HARMONIC SERIES

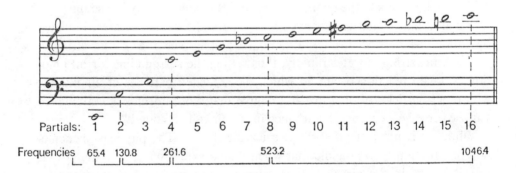

A sound is perceived as musical when the spectrum of the sound shows strong harmonic partials and few, or very weak, inharmonic partials. Conversely, a sound is perceived as noise when the spectrum of the sound reveals many, or strong, inharmonic partials. The following diagrams illustrate the difference between the sound waves of noise and a musical tone. Notice that regular, repetitive patterns appear in the sound wave of a musical tone, while there is no regularity whatsoever in the noise sound wave.

NOISE AND MUSICAL TONE

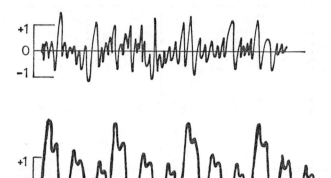

The reason all musical instruments do not sound alike is that each of their spectra is different. In other words, we can distinguish between musical tones because of the varying numbers and strengths of the particular harmonic partials that occur within each tone.

In the diagram on the following page, you can see that the tone of a tuning fork has a single partial while the tone of an oboe has several partials, the strongest being its fourth and fifth partials. The spectrum of a musical tone produced by a horn is quite different from the spectra produced by either the tuning fork or the oboe. The musical tone of a horn includes a strong first partial and several upper partials which diminish gradually in intensity. It differs noticeably from a musical tone produced by a flute, which contains a weak first partial and an extremely strong and distinguishing second partial located one octave above the fundamental (first partial). (On the diagram, octaves are indicated by the broken lines.)

SPECTRA OF TUNING FORK, OBOE, HORN, AND FLUTE

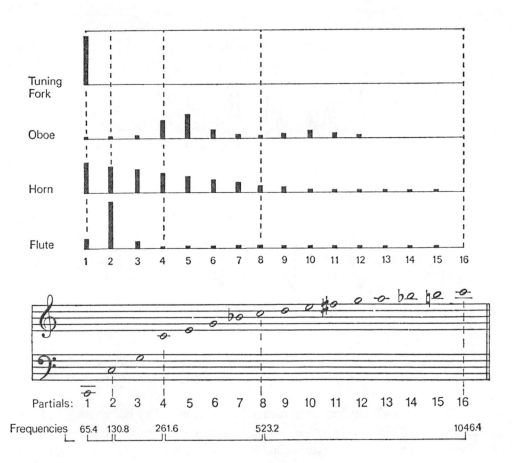

If you have access to a piano, you can demonstrate for yourself the mathematical relationship of harmonics. The first of the following demonstrations illustrates that the second partial of a given musical sound is one octave above the first partial (fundamental). The second demonstration illustrates that the fourth partial of a musical sound is two octaves above the fundamental. The final demonstration is an exercise in inharmonics in which there is no mathematical relationship between the pitches.

EXPERIMENT 1:

Go to the piano and hold down the C_4 (middle C), thus releasing the damper in the back so that the string of C_4 can vibrate freely. Let the sound die out, but keep the damper open by continuing to keep the key depressed. Then quickly strike C_3 (one octave lower), but do not use the sustaining pedal. Its sound will be percussive and short. The sound of C_3 will die out immediately, but since you are still holding down C_4, you should hear the vibration of C_4.

Try the procedure again, listening carefully for the harmonic—the vibration of C_4. C_3 is the first partial, and C_4 the second partial. C_4 "sings out" because of the effect of sympathetic vibration. The pitch C_4 is the second partial of the complex sound wave created by the C_3 string (tuned to 131 hertz). Since the C_4 string, which is tuned to 262 hertz, is open and free to vibrate, it responds from sympathetic vibratory action to the second partial of C_3.

Notice that octaves are related in a ratio of two to one. If a note has 100 vibrations per second (hertz), the same note one octave higher will have 200 hertz. Two octaves higher it will have 400 hertz; three octaves higher, 800 hertz, etc.

EXPERIMENT 2:

For a second demonstration of harmonics, hold down C_5 instead of C_4. Strike C_3. Listen for C_5, the fourth harmonic. You may have to listen more carefully to hear the harmonic "sing out," because pianos vary and the sound may be weaker. (See chart on following page.)

EXPERIMENT 3:

For a third demonstration, strike C_4 while holding down D_5 (one octave and a note above C_4) to discover whether the D_5 pitch is part of the overtone series of middle C_4. Since it is NOT, the D_5 pitch will not "sing out" sympathetically because it is not in the overtone series of the C_4 pitch. D_5 is *INHARMONIC* to C_4.

HARMONIC STRUCTURES OF DIFFERENT PIANOS

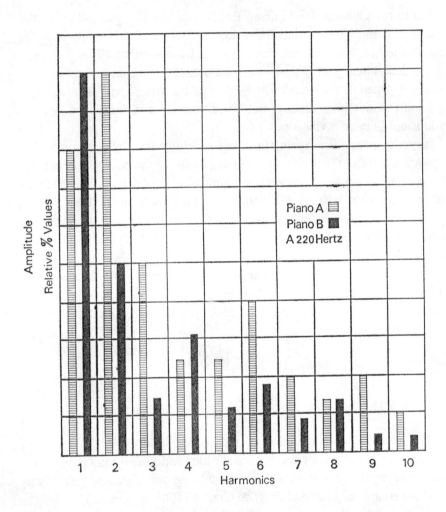

You might enjoy experimenting with some of the other pitches in the harmonic series. If so, refer back to the diagram of the harmonic series on page 62, follow the procedures used in the three preceding demonstrations, and discover the various pitches that are harmonic to one another.

White noise—such as the sound of the surf, the wind, or the noise a TV makes when the channel is off the air—is comprised of a spectrum which includes all pitches (within a certain band) at random frequencies and random amplitudes. In white noise there is no evidence of any regular harmonic partial series. Perhaps it is called "white" noise because the color "white" includes all colors in its spectrum. We produce white noise when we say, "Shhhh," to remind our children to be quiet.

Although most consonants in singing contain many inharmonic partials, singers can produce vowels with clearly defined overtone structures containing few, if any, inharmonic partials. Most people label the resulting quality of sound "musical." It is sound that is free from distortion and dissonance, is attractive, pleasing, round, full, and rich. A major goal of all serious singers is to be able to produce a "musical" tone on vowels.

Singing is sustained speech, an extension of speech, but with musical modification. THE DIFFERENCE BETWEEN SPEECH AND SINGING IS THAT THE VOWELS OF SPEECH HAVE MANY INHARMONIC PARTIALS, WHILE IN SINGING THEY SHOULD NOT!

Noise

A certain amount of NOISE is produced in every instrument—the plucking sounds of stringed instruments, the clatter of valves in wind instruments, the rush of breath used in the attack of the sound, and the consonants in texts of songs. All these sounds and noises are produced by the number and strength of the inharmonic partials present in the tone.

In the vocal instrument, inharmonic partials occur in the formation of most consonants and in tones produced with vocal constriction or breathiness. In skillful singing, however, the amount of noise is controlled and utilized consciously to enhance the literary, emotional, and musical aspects of the song.

Excessive use of inharmonic partials is usually a result of poor vocal technique and is an annoying distraction to the listener. Vocal constriction (hypertension) produces such unpleasant noises as gasping sounds, raspy intakes of breath, throatiness and strained sound on the vowels (where, technically, there is no necessity for noise). A certain amount of noise will be produced by consonants because that is the nature of language, but this normal noise will not be offensive unless it is excessive, produced incorrectly, or used inappropriately for the language.

Some singers utilize excessive noise quite consciously and successfully for purposes of style. Consider the recorded breathy sounds of Nancy Wilson and the gravelly voice of Louis Armstrong. These two singers use unique sounds to create their distinctive styles. Other singers such as Robert Merrill,

Joan Sutherland, and Beverly Sills have trained their voices to create strong harmonic partials and the least noise possible, because such purity of sound is demanded in their operatic style of singing.

We become accustomed to the inharmonic partials produced by all musical instruments, and frequently, instead of finding the noise unpleasant, we begin to like it or else we ignore it. Have you ever noticed the noise made by a classical guitarist when he plays his instrument? Sometimes it may bother us at first, but usually we either tune it out or come to accept it as an integral part of the sound of that particular instrument.

A piano makes noise when the hammer strikes the strings and when the pedals are pushed. Sometimes the keys themselves clatter, but most of us do not even "hear" it. The harpsichord (the predecessor of the piano) actuates the vibration of its strings by a plucking movement which produces a very distinct noise that is quite audible to contemporary ears. When the piano was invented, however, Johann Sebastian Bach and his contemporaries complained bitterly about the amount of noise it produced! Bach said the piano would never be a successful musical instrument because of its excessive noise. Surprisingly, he was not disturbed by the noise of the harpsichord. In fact, he didn't "hear" any!

No one instrument performs perfectly on all counts; instead, each instrument is useful and valuable because of its particular contribution. With a musical saw, for example, accurate pitch is difficult to achieve and sustain, but this is compensated by the fact that a musical saw has a most interesting tone quality which makes itself valuable within its limited potential.

Although everyone has certain boundaries in their physical characteristics, all of us possess the same essential vocal equipment. Your instrument is not equipped differently from mine; nor is mine better than yours; they both have the same basic ingredients. Since we are not limited by the components of our instrument, the quality of performance rests upon our skill as a singer and the healthful and musical use of our vocal instrument. The vocal instrument responds to the will and skill of the performer.

CHAPTER FIVE

MORE ABOUT MUSIC

* * *

"NUCLEAR BOMBS"

Joan has a disconcerting penchant for casually dropping "nuclear bombs" into my placid existence. For example, the day before my second singing lesson, she called me up on the demon telephone and said, sweetly: "Let's drive up to TWU (Texas Woman's University) early tomorrow morning and we'll hold your voice lesson in my studio. I have made arrangements to videotape your lesson there."

Videotape, I thought to myself. Good grief, that's television! Sound and picture! All my budding confidence as a novice student of singing vanished in a flood of fear. Upon picking myself up off the floor, I managed to inquire, somewhat hysterically, "Why?"

"Well," she said, matter-of-factly, "by recording a beginning lesson now, we can better evaluate your present status. Later we will be able to determine exactly what progress you've made. It will also be helpful for me to have an opportunity to observe myself teaching. The arrangements are all made. Ray will bring his video equipment to my studio tomorrow morning at nine o'clock."

Realizing that I was outfoxed, outclassed, and outsmarted, I shrugged my shoulders in resignation, gritted my teeth and agreed to the inevitable. Can a woman "gird her loins" like the biblical men of old? If so, I suspect I did.

If it hadn't been for the unexpected videotaping factor, I would have looked forward to the second lesson with anticipation and a fair amount of confidence. The interim week of home practice sessions had been fun. The "Ohm" chants were relaxing and I was beginning to feel more secure in producing high and low notes. The element of fear that had dominated my thoughts prior to the first lesson had dissipated. Practicing twice daily with the aid of a cassette tape prepared by Joan (in which she structured the practice session and demonstrated desired responses) had been a positive, confidence-building experience.

At nine o'clock the following morning, Joan and I and Ray and his TV equipment assembled in Joan's studio. I was very conscious of the presence of Ray and his camera until about ten minutes into the lesson, when I forgot all about them. Joan, a seasoned performer, seemed to be unconscious of the camera altogether.

The lesson consisted of working with vowels while performing exercises which help to extend vocal range and to produce easy, free, unconstricted sounds. We also worked on whispering vowels with the mouth in various positions.

Almost before I knew it, the thirty-minute lesson had sped by and it was time to view the videotape. Much to my amazement, I heard myself actually producing some pleasant singing sounds while performing the high/low vowel exercises. I was most struck, though, by the pleasant quality of my speaking voice. For years I have labored under the misconception that I spoke in a decided monotone. I was totally convinced that I spoke in a dull, flat drone until I heard with my own ears an attractive, melodious speaking voice emanating from the soundtrack. And it was MINE!

During our third voice lesson, any remaining notions about my monotone speaking voice were dispelled when we tape-recorded my voice to determine whether I was speaking in my proper pitch range. The pleasant speaking voice qualities again shone through. I couldn't help but think that if singing truly is sustained speech, then perhaps I will someday be able to carry over the good speaking qualities into attractive singing. What a delightful thought!

Practice sessions at home have become an experience I look forward to each day. For one thing, it assures me of thirty minutes of absolute privacy. Whenever the "time for practice" gleam lights in my eyes, my children discreetly vanish. All I have to do is look in the direction of my cassette tape recorder and my children do a disappearing act. It works every time. Sometimes the family dog doesn't make it out of the room before the door closes behind the escape artists. But he knows. He slinks over into the farthest corner, curls up into a ball, places both front paws over his head, and whines pitifully throughout the practice period. However, I will show no mercy to that family of mine; I shall persevere! At least until the day the dog decides to sit on my head while I lie on the floor attempting to achieve proper breathing responses.

RICKY

RHYTHM AND TEMPO IN MUSIC

Rhythm . . . "covers the ensemble of everything pertaining to what may be called the time side of music (as distinct from the pitch side), i.e. it takes in beats, accents, measures or bars, grouping of notes into beats, grouping of beats into measures, grouping of measures into phrases, and so forth."*

Rhythm is the organization of sound in time. In music, the term "time" includes two different aspects—first, the DURATION of a single sound; and secondly, the TEMPO or overall speed of the music (how fast or how slowly the music goes). Rhythm is the organization of single notes into groups to form patterns. This can be done rigidly or with considerable flexibility.

Almost all beginning singers (and almost everyone else as well!) respond naturally to songs containing a strong, regular pulsation, because these songs seem to stimulate feelings of security and a sense of order.

In the excellent book entitled *Music in Therapy,* long considered the "Bible" of music therapists, E. Thayer Gaston, editor, writes:

When the musics from all the cultures of the world are considered, it is rhythm that stands out as most fundamental. Rhythm is the organizer and the energizer. Without rhythm, there would be no music, whereas there is much music that has neither melody nor harmony. Combinations of rhythm, melody, harmony and counterpoint have been in existence less than one thousand years, but rhythm has been the music of millions for many thousands of years. It is rhythm alone that makes possible the temporal order of music. For most people it is rhythm that provides the energy of music, be it small or great. The unique potential of rhythm to energize and bring order will be seen as the most influential factor of music.*

It is now known that man relates to rhythm even before birth. In a recent recording by Dr. Hajime Murooka ("Lullabies from the Womb," Capitol ⅜ST-11421, 1974 edition), one can hear the actual regular, pulsating sounds which are heard by the fetus while still in the womb. The sounds, which are

* Percy A. Scholes, *The Oxford Companion to Music* (Oxford University Press, 1974), p. 872.
* Macmillan Co., 1968, p. 17.

surprisingly loud, are the sounds of the pulsation of blood through the mother's veins and arteries, rather than the sound of her heartbeat, which used to be considered the primary noise of the fetal environment. The regular, pulsating sounds heard in the womb closely resemble the sound of industrial machinery. If Dr. Murooka's recording is played to a fretful newborn, the infant will calm down and be comforted, and will soon fall asleep! This same comforting regularity of sound continues during an infant's early life when his mother rocks him to sleep while she hums or croons a lullaby. Lullabies, incidentally, are similar the world over. Not only are they repetitious in rhythm, but they are usually accompanied by gentle rocking.

Rhythm occurs when individual sounds of a specific duration are combined in an orderly and repetitious manner. When this organization is metric (has a constant, repetitious pattern), the rhythm is described as strong and pulsing and is indicative of most dance and primitive music, including folk songs and tribal music. However, this type of music is not necessarily always simple in construction. In addition to strong, pulsing rhythms, the drum music of Africa displays a highly intricate organization of rhythmical patterns.

According to Gaston (p. 18), rhythm is not only . . .

the chief factor in the organization of music, it is, generally speaking, the chief energizer—the primitive, driving factor in music. When rhythm is enunciated by detached, percussive sounds, it stimulates muscular action, particularly if there is some variation in the rhythmic pattern. When we think of the music of preliterate people, it is percussive in nature; it calls up visions of strenuous physical action. The drum is the best instrument for such dances, just as it is the best instrument for marching. But percussive music may also be the product of other instruments, the piano for example. Whenever the dance in unrestrained and uninhibited, the accompaniment is percussive and highly rhythmical. The basic dynamic factor of dance bands is the rhythm section.

The opposite reaction is found to melodic passages in which rhythm is at a minimum and the sounds are nonpercussive and legato. There is far less physical movement. A typical adagio movement such as that in the "Divertimento" by Mozart actually curtails movement. It seems to induce a contemplative response. Sustained, nonrhythmical music makes no demand for physical activity, but rather induces esthetic fantasy.

Although all music exists on a continuum, striking contrasts in response to the two extremes can be observed in our everyday life. The behavior of adolescent dancers could not be what it is if nonpercussive music were used. Church congregations respond differently to the organ from the way they do to the piano. At concerts the most rhythmical music is played last so the applause will be greater. Generally, the finest legato music receives less applause than, for example, "Bolero" by Ravel.

The effect of the lullaby and hypnogenetic music derives from a monotonously regular and mildly accented type of rhythm in which there is little or no variation.

All functional lullabies are unrelenting in rhythm; even the well-known "Berceuse" of Chopin has not the slightest variation in the basic rhythm supporting the melody.

The behavior of groups of people as well as that of individuals can often be controlled by the type of music used. It is the amount of rhythm and the manner in which the rhythm is indicated that determine, in large part, the amount of energy invested in the physical response to music. The "startle response" occurs only to percussive sound.†

If one wished, for example, to establish a meditative mood or Alpha level of consciousness, he could listen to nonpercussive music such as Zen *ragas* and gentle melodic music without percussivity or large dynamic contrasts.

Most of today's pop music so favored by young people bears striking similarities to the regular rhythms found in prenatal and infant life. Actually, these similarities are not limited to adolescents. They are the basic rhythms of life to which all people of all ages cannot help but respond.

Most people of Western cultural orientation must make a conscious effort to understand what is taking place in some contemporary art music. Since it is our natural inclination "not to enjoy" music to which we cannot tap our toe, we may have to work hard at first if we are to find pleasure in music that seems to be lacking in obvious or traditional rhythmic order. Once the less easily defined rhythm of "new music" is perceived, the listener needs to develop a new awareness and an increased interest in form and tone color, rather than in melody and harmony. Form and tone color are the major expressional elements of new music.

The more knowledgeable we become musically, the more interested we become in these other aspects of music . . . instead of depending upon the comfortable metronomic regularity of beat. As our musical horizons broaden, we learn to listen with intellectual awareness, emotive pleasure, and an increased comprehension of new rhythmic structures, pitch, dynamics, tone color, and form. We learn to respond to larger musical forms, longer melodic patterns and phrases, and longer, less obvious rhythmical patterns. Thus we find ourselves understanding and enjoying music that is primarily composed of juxtapositions of varying tone colors written for the purpose of creating musical form and emotional effect.

The Musical Notation of Rhythm and Tempo

The duration of a single sound in music is called the TIME of that sound. Since time can be measured by instruments (like a clock), the duration of

† Ibid.

any musical sound can be measured in terms of how long the sound lasts . . . whether for four seconds, half a second, or whatever.

In music, each sound is measured in actual and relative time. That is, each sound can be measured by the clock in actual time and can also be measured by its relative duration to other sounds. In written music, the various kinds of sounds always have a mathematical relationship to one another.

Each sound in music is indicated by a symbol called a NOTE. Each note indicates a specific duration of time and is placed on a musical staff to indicate a specific pitch. As mentioned above, notes in music indicate both actual and relative time, the relative time being more significant because it is always consistent mathematically whereas the tempo and time signature (rhythmical groupings) will change.

The following represents some of the various notes, their names and their relative time values:

Relative Time Value of Notes

○ Whole note

♩ Half note   ½ the time of a whole note;
                       twice the time of a quarter note.

♩ Quarter note   ¼ the time of a whole note;
                       ½ the time of a half note;
                       twice the time of an eighth note.

♪ Eighth note   ⅛ the time of a whole note;
                       ½ the time of a quarter note;
                       twice the time of a sixteenth note.

♪ Sixteenth note $\frac{1}{16}$ the time of a whole note;
                       ½ the time of an eighth note.

A logical question follows: "How long does the whole note last?" The answer is that it varies from song to song, depending upon the chosen TEMPO of the song. Arbitrarily, for each song, we assign a duration of time to the whole note which will remain constant in a song until a change is indicated in the score. In one song the whole note might have a duration of four full seconds, and in another song the whole note might last for only two seconds. But the relative time of the whole, the half, and the quarter notes is AL-WAYS constant. For example:

If the whole note [𝅝] = 4 full seconds,

then the half note [𝅗𝅥] = 2 full seconds,

the quarter note [𝅘𝅥] = 1 full second,

the eighth note [𝅘𝅥𝅮] = ½ second,

and the sixteenth note [𝅘𝅥𝅯] = ¼ second.

A composer needs a method for communicating the tempo he desires for his song. He accomplishes this through various words and/or symbols placed at the top of the first line of the song. The most effective method is a metronome marking which looks like this: ♩=60.

A metronome is a mechanical device which gives a certain number of audible strokes or clicks per minute. Sixty means you will hear 60 clicks per minute. One hundred twenty would mean 120 clicks per minute (a typical march tempo). ♩=60 indicates there will be 60 quarter notes per minute, or one quarter note per second. (How convenient that there are 60 seconds in a minute!) We don't even have to own a metronome to use this marking method to set our tempo; instead we can substitute the second hand of a wristwatch to estimate the speed.

♩=60 would be a likely marking for the songs:

"Swing Low"
"Nobody Knows the Trouble I've Seen"
"Were You There?"

Another method used by composers to communicate tempo is through written instructions (i.e., fast, slow, moderate, *allegro, adagio, lento,* or *presto*). Sometimes the composer gives no specification at all, and the performer is free to select his own tempo. Occasionally, a descriptive word denoting an emotion will assist in determining appropriate pace (for instance, "sadly" might suggest a slow tempo).

Music is made up not only of sound, but of *silence*—each silence lasting for a specific duration. A silence in music is referred to as a REST. Rests, which are relative in time to notes, are depicted like this:

Whole rest	▬
Half rest	▬
Quarter rest	𝄽
Eighth rest	𝄾
Sixteenth rest	𝄿

MUSICAL NOTATION

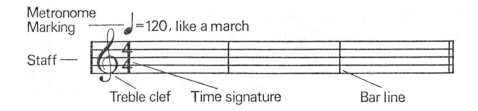

Treble clef   Time signature   Bar line

Rhythm Exercises

RHYTHM is the grouping of sounds into patterns that are ordered by a basic underlying beat. Each time a musician learns a new piece of music, he always begins by discovering the basic underlying beat (pulse) of the music. Next, he arranges the individual notes into orderly patterns that are delineated by the basic beat.

Beginning musicians often fail to maintain a steady, regular beat if they simply tap their hand or foot. However, if they walk-out a pattern, the forward motion of their body assists in keeping the steps (beats) regular and constant.

EXERCISE 1:

PURPOSE: To establish a regular, basic underlying beat by walking-out a series of steady, ongoing, repetitive steps.

Simply walk around the room in order to establish a solid, regular beat which will be maintained in the forthcoming rhythm exercises. Walk at a medium speed, using a steady pace. Continue walking until you feel you have established a regular beat.

NOTE: The equal duration of each walking step will be represented visually by symbols placed equidistant on the page. In the diagrams presented throughout this series of exercises, each footprint symbol indicates one step (one beat).

Example:

Step   Step   Step   Step

EXERCISE 2:

PURPOSE: To establish groups of basic beats into orderly repetitive patterns.

A. As you continue to walk around the room, try to conceive of the steps belonging to groups of four steps each. You can distinguish the groups from one another by accenting the first step in each set of four steps. (Accent the first step by making it slightly louder than the three succeeding steps in each group.) KEEP ALL STEPS EVEN IN DURATION. The accented step should not last any longer than the unaccented steps. Don't pause between groups.

Example:

Groups of Four.

	1	2	3	4		1	2	3	4		1	2	3	4
Walk this Basic Beat:														

NOTE: In written music, straight vertical lines (called BAR LINES) are used to divide music into MEASURES (groups of beats). A measure is the space between each bar line. An ACCENTED BEAT usually occurs at the beginning of a measure, but not always. When you are walking the rhythm exercises, don't pause at the bar line. Continue walking in steps of even duration in order to establish an ongoing, steady rhythm.

Example:

Groups of Four.

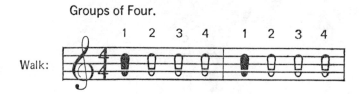

B. The diagrams below represent basic musical rhythm patterns. Walk-out each pattern, accenting the steps indicated by dark footprints.

Examples:

Groups of Two.

Groups of Three.

Groups of Four.

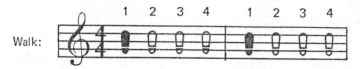

Walk:

Groups of Six.

Walk:

C. In addition to the more steady types of rhythmical patterns, much of today's music incorporates odd-numbered patterns of beats (five, seven, nine) and alternating beat patterns. Walk-out the following rhythmical patterns, keeping the steps EVEN!

Example:

Groups of Two-Three.

Groups of Five.

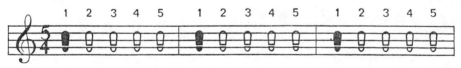

Groups of Three-Four.

EXERCISE 3:

PURPOSE: To develop skills in co-ordinating singing with basic beats.

A. While walking-out the rhythm patterns indicated below, sing the sound "ta," using a comfortable pitch and a steady volume.

Example:

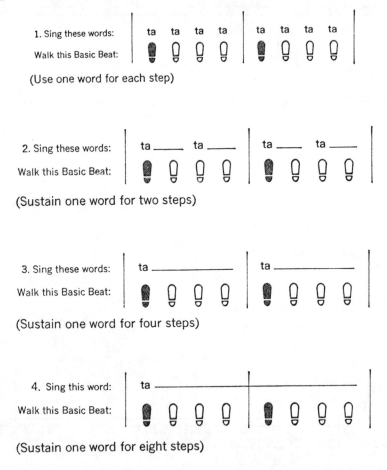

1. Sing these words: ta   ta   ta   ta | ta   ta   ta   ta

   Walk this Basic Beat:

   (Use one word for each step)

2. Sing these words: ta ____ ta ____ | ta ____ ta ____

   Walk this Basic Beat:

   (Sustain one word for two steps)

3. Sing these words: ta _____ | ta _____

   Walk this Basic Beat:

   (Sustain one word for four steps)

4. Sing this word: ta _____

   Walk this Basic Beat:

   (Sustain one word for eight steps)

B. Practice different combinations of sounds and steps. All of these examples group the basic beats into patterns of four steps. These exercises are basically body co-ordination exercises, designed to develop the skill of doing two rhythms simultaneously, one walking and another singing.

1. Use a moderate, walking tempo for the basic beat.

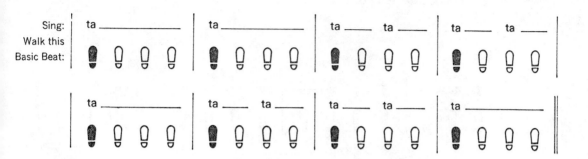

2. Use a moderate tempo for the basic beat.

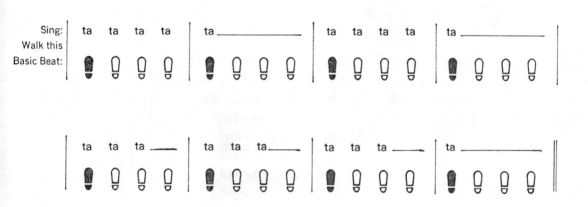

3. Since silence is also an integral part of music, be silent wherever indicated by the notation [𝄽] for "rests." Use a moderate tempo.

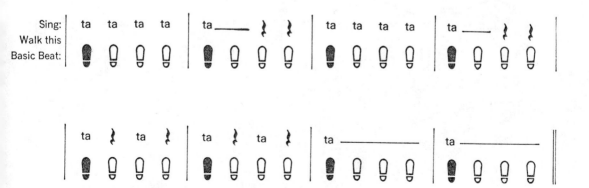

4. Use a moderate tempo.

5. The curved lines above the "ta's" indicate a musical phrase and suggest a place to breathe (B). Use a SLOW tempo for the basic beat in this exercise.

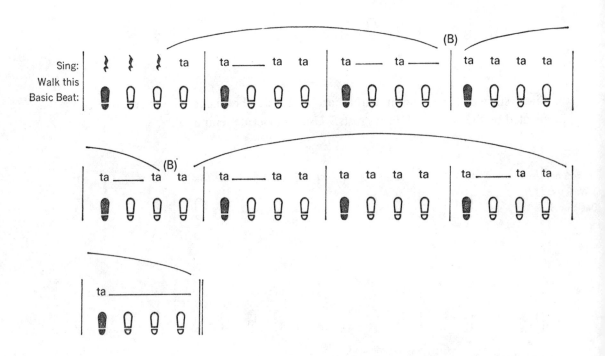

6. Use a SLOW basic beat.

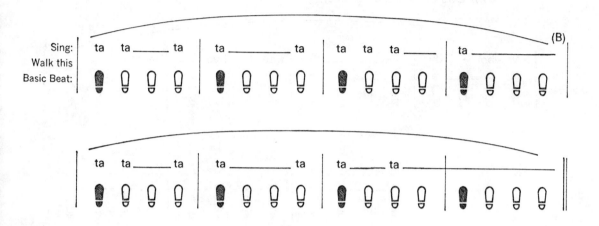

7. Use a FAST basic beat.

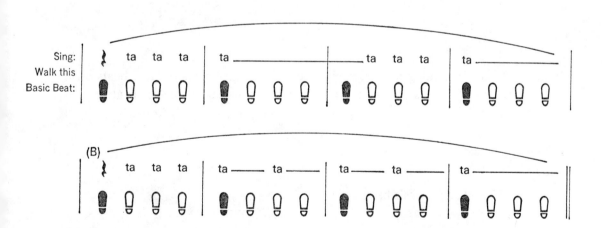

NOTE: In the above examples, the singing sounds of part 5 formed the rhythm of the first line of the familiar song, *O Come, All Ye Faithful*, part 6 was *Nobody Knows the Trouble I've Seen*, part 7 was *When the Saints Go Marching In*.

Example:

Nobody Knows the Trouble I've Seen

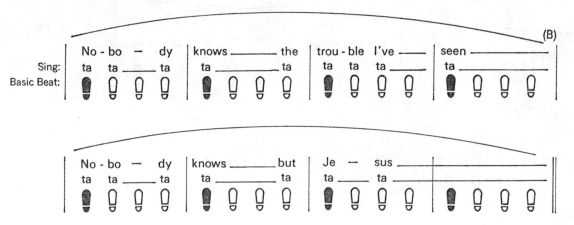

In the remaining portion of the exercise, the groupings of basic beats form patterns of three steps (counts). Give a slight accent to the first beat in each measure.

8. Use a SLOW basic beat.

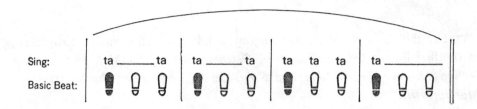

9. Use a FAST basic beat.

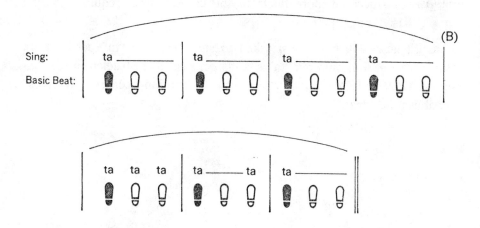

10. Use a FAST basic beat.

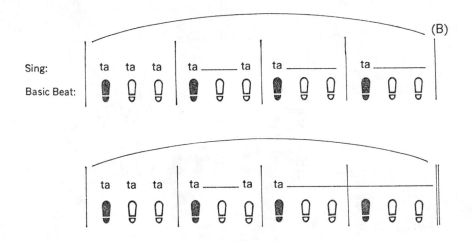

NOTE: In the above examples, the singing sounds of part 8 formed the rhythm of *We Three Kings*, part 9 was the line "Daisy, Daisy, give me your answer true" from *Bicycle Built for Two*, and part 10 was *After the Ball Is Over!*

EXERCISE 4:

PURPOSE: To become more facile in the co-ordination required to sing rhythmical patterns.

Until now, you have been asked to sing only one "ta" per beat. In this exercise, sing multiple "ta" sounds per beat as instructed in the diagram. Be sure to keep your steps even in duration because the "steps" establish the "beat."

Example:

1. Moderate tempo

(Counts)	1	2	3	4		1	2	3	4
Sing:	ta ta	ta ta	ta ___			ta ta	ta ta	ta ___	
Basic Beat:	👣	👣	👣	👣		👣	👣	👣	👣

2. Moderate tempo

(Counts)	1	2	3	4		1	2	3	4
Sing:	ta ___ ta	ta ta ___	ta ta			ta ___ ta	ta ta	___	
Basic Beat:	👣	👣	👣	👣		👣	👣	👣	👣

3. Moderate tempo

(Counts)	1	2	3	4		1	2	3	4
Sing:	ta ___	ta ta	___ ta			ta ___	ta ta	___	
Basic Beat:	👣	👣	👣	👣		👣	👣	👣	👣

4. Moderate tempo

(Counts)	1	2	3	4		1	2	3	4
Sing:	ta ta ___	ta ta ___				ta ta ___	ta ta ta		
Basic Beat:	👣	👣	👣	👣		👣	👣	👣	👣

SYNCOPATION (emphasizing a rhythm that occurs "off the beat") is a rhythmical device found in much contemporary music (especially jazz and dance music). It lends a very different kind of energy and emotion to a musical expression in comparison with music that is "on the beat." You can experience syncopation by alternately tapping the table with your hand (establishing a basic beat) and snapping your fingers (syncopating the beat). Repeat the two actions in a repetitive, regular, recurring rhythm.

Example:

TAP–SNAP–TAP–SNAP–TAP–SNAP
Now, say "ta" on the snap. This creates vocal syncopation.

Example:

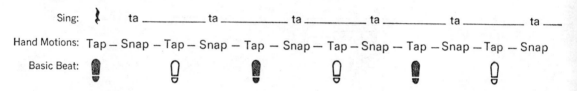

NOTE: In musical notation, the basic beat and its pattern are designated by two numbers located at the beginning of each piece of music. These numbers offer specific and necessary information for the performance of the composition.

Example:

Each TOP number indicates the number of beats (counts) per measure.

Example:

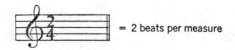 = 2 beats per measure

The BOTTOM number indicates the type of note which gets one beat. If you place an imaginary "1" over the bottom number in the above example (4), it makes a fraction (¼) which indicates that a quarter note will get one beat in this particular piece of music.

In summary, then, the 2/4 notation of time tells us that this piece of music has two beats to a measure and that a quarter note gets one beat.

Example:

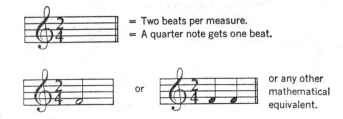

3/4 means that there are three beats to a measure and that a quarter note gets one beat.

Example:

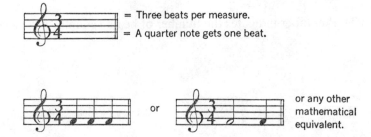

And 6/8 means that there are six beats to a measure and an eighth note gets one beat.

Example:

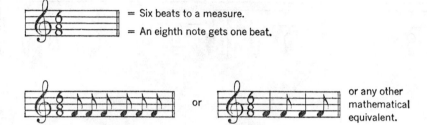

Practice these examples. (Remember that each note or rest has a specific time value and indicates the duration of sound and silence. Refer back to pages 74, 75, and 76 for note and rest values.)

Example:

1. Moderate tempo

2. Moderate tempo

3. Fast tempo

4. Fast Tempo

5. Slow tempo

6. Moderate tempo

DYNAMICS IN MUSIC

In music, the term "dynamics" simply means how loudly or softly we produce the sound. By varying the degree of loudness within a single phrase (in singing, from one breath to another), or from one note to another, or even while sustaining a single note, the musician gives shape, emphasis, energy, emotion, style, shading, and color to the music. The artistic use of dynamics, therefore, becomes a major element in musical expression and communication.

The musical terms "intensity" and "volume" are also used frequently to refer to loudness. Although these two terms are often used interchangeably, they do not refer to exactly the same thing. INTENSITY, which can be measured, refers to the energy of a sound wave and is measured by the amplitude of the sound wave (see below). VOLUME refers to the loudness or softness of sound as perceived by the listener. As we shall discover later, the volume the listener perceives is not always the same as the actual degree of measurable intensity.

PITCH AT MEDIUM INTENSITY

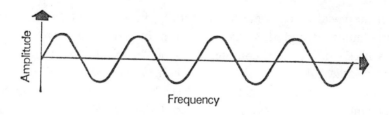

PITCH AT LOUDER INTENSITY

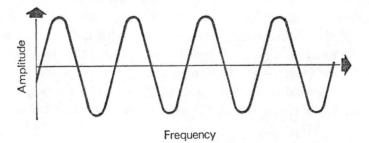

Dynamics in the Voice

Physically, within the voice, the loudness or softness of a tone results from the amount of air directed toward the vocal cords and from the usage of the resonating cavities. Primarily, volume is controlled by the amount of breath pressure and the adjustment of the vocal cords.

On lower pitches, the vocal cords are usually thicker and contribute to louder volumes by increasing in tension and thickness as the air pressure is increased. Since the cords become thinner to produce higher pitches (as in a man's falsetto), more air flow (breath) is needed to produce louder volume. When singing softly, the vocal cords become thinner and less tense; when singing loudly, they thicken and become more tense.

All of these laryngeal adjustments occur automatically, in direct response to the singer's mental image of the sound he wishes to produce and his controlled breath pressure. In other words, four laryngeal elements work together to create pitch, volume, and tone color in response to our mental images. The four elements of the vocal cords are: length, thickness, mass, and tension. What is of particular interest to the student of voice is that the musculature of the larynx can actually develop increased flexibility and strength through correct usage over a period of time. Practice does make perfect!

When the vocal cords come together fully, in an orderly fashion, breathiness is eliminated and the carrying power of a tone is increased. Thus, a well-voiced soft tone is considered to be "efficient" because it can be heard in a large hall much more easily than an energetic but breathy tone. (A breathy tone occurs when the vocal cords do not come together firmly, thus allowing air to escape.) A well-voiced tone is said to have "carrying power." The singer must select an appropriate degree of voicing to achieve the desired musical effect. For instance, if he is using a microphone and desires to convey a sense of intimacy, he may choose to use breathy tones.

Other major factors which affect the volume of a tone are the shape and usage of the singer's resonating cavities (the mouth and throat and, occasionally, the nasal passages). Of the two prominent resonators (the mouth and throat), the mouth is the more movable. The shape of the resonators is determined by an individual's physical structure and by the way he enunciates vowels. Vowel enunciation is the more significant factor because skillful enunciation is directly related to the development of greater skills in amplification. There is a direct correlation between the way a singer shapes his vowels on various pitches and the degree of amplification (resonance) he achieves. A singer's mouth literally performs like a megaphone.

In summary, the three ways in which we can physically increase our control of volume are: 1. using breath properly; 2. strengthening and maintaining flexibility of the vocal cords; and 3. increasing vowel production skills in order to achieve optimum resonance.

Dynamics in Song

Every song contains dynamic levels within it which are particularly suited to its most effective interpretation. The singer is asked to consciously select, from a wide range of possible loudness levels, those which seem most appropriate for any given song. Let's experiment with some songs to see the different ways in which dynamics are used.

LOUDNESS CAN VARY FROM NOTE TO NOTE. When singing the following song ("Waltzing Matilda"), sing percussively, using a strong rhythmical beat, almost like a march. Notice the difference in loudness on some individual notes when they are accented (sung more loudly) to achieve and appropriate quality of lighthearted gusto.

WALTZING MATILDA

With an easy swing . . . light and gay

Waltz-ing Ma-til-da,   Waltz-ing Ma-til-da,   You'll come a-waltz-ing Ma - til - da with   me.

Where's that jol-ly   jum-buck You've got in your tuck-er bag? You'll come a-waltz-ing Ma-til-da with me.

jumbuck . . . a sheep
tucker . . . food

LOUDNESS CAN VARY FROM ONE PHRASE TO ANOTHER, EITHER GRADUALLY OR ABRUPTLY. In this song, sing the melody in a lyrical, flowing, expansive manner.

O COME, ALL YE FAITHFUL

Notice that you probably sang the underlined phrases more loudly than the other phrases of the song. These are climactic (especially significant) phrases. In both cases the pitches are higher. Singers often elect to make an *allargando* (a slowing down) at the end of the song. This adds emphasis, in the same way an increase in loudness does.

AN ENTIRE SONG WILL OFTEN VARY DRAMATICALLY IN VOLUME FROM ANOTHER SONG. Reflective songs, such as these, are sung most effectively when using a soft level of dynamics:

"Close to You," by Burt Bacharach
"Summertime," from *Porgy and Bess* by George Gershwin
"Kum Ba Ya," a Nigerian Folk Song
"Depuis le Jour," from *Louise* by Gustave Charpentier

On a ten-point scale, with the rating of one representing the softest singing and ten the loudest, all of the above songs would rate less than five.

However, the following songs, exuberant in nature, would all have ratings of five or above:

"Oklahoma," from *Oklahoma* by Richard Rodgers and Oscar Hammer-
  stein
"Joy to the World," by George F. Handel
"Mack the Knife," from *The Threepenny Opera* by Kurt Weill
"Toreador Song," from *Carmen* by Georges Bizet

Some songs demand greater variations in dynamic levels within the song to be effective and to achieve proper style. Others need little or no variation. VARIATION refers to such techniques as the swelling of a single note, long crescendos or diminuendos, and quick, abrupt changes in loudness.

Most concert literature (art songs, opera, oratorio) requires considerable variation in dynamic levels. However, concert music from the Baroque period is exceptional in that it does not utilize *gradual* changes in volume levels. Instead, it is distinguished by *sudden* changes that imitated the popular keyboard instrument of that time (the harpsichord, which did not have the subtle capability for making gradual dynamic changes).

Folk songs, by contrast, traditionally do not use crescendos and diminuendos. Wide variations in dynamic levels within a song are inappropriate to this style of music.

The use of electronic equipment for amplification also influences sung dynamic levels. A singer can sing rather softly, yet gain considerable amplification through the use of a good sound system. When singing over a microphone, the singer must be certain that the speaker system is placed in such a fashion that he can monitor his sound and know precisely what volume and quality the audience is hearing. Otherwise, he has no artistic control or he must rely on the opinions of others—something that is never wise to do because it restricts spontaneous creative expression.

I have personally experienced the problems encountered in recording sessions when the dynamic levels are manipulated by an electronics engineer who is not a musician. While singing for the finals of the Metropolitan Opera Auditions of the Air (performing "Non so più, cosa son, cosa faccio" from Mozart's *Marriage of Figaro*), I deliberately used considerable volume in certain passages and sang softly in others. My performance was to be judged by a tape made at the New York studio, but the engineer (who had worked diligently to keep the dynamic levels EVEN) had softened the louder passages and bolstered the softer ones! This resulted in a recording that had almost no variety or shading and dynamics levels that remained constant throughout the aria. Quite different from how it had actually been sung!

Such a situation can produce a major problem in nightclub work if the amplifier is controlled by a club manager who is unaware of the singer's problems. Also, if the volume of the instrumental music is too high, or if the speakers are placed at such an angle that the singer has difficulty hearing himself, he usually compensates by singing more loudly, with the result that he taxes his voice and loses subtlety and control over his song.

MUSICAL NOTATION FOR DYNAMICS

Composers and editors utilize the markings listed below to indicate the dynamics they desire in the performance of their songs. The markings are written within the context of the song, usually from measure to measure, but sometimes even from note to note.

MUSICAL NOTATION

pp	*pianissimo*	very soft
p	*piano*	soft
mp	*mezzo piano*	moderately soft
mf	*mezzo forte*	moderately loud
f	*forte*	loud
ff	*fortissimo*	very loud
sf (>)	*sforzando*	immediately loud on a single note
sub p	*subito piano*	immediately softer
<	*crescendo*	increasingly louder
>	*diminuendo*	increasingly softer

INTENSITY AND VOLUME

The measurable versus perceptual element of loudness is an interesting phenomenon because the actual measurable loudness (intensity) is not always the same as the perceived loudness (volume). If we play two notes on a piano simultaneously, the *C* two octaves below middle *C* (a man's low *C*) and another note four octaves higher (a woman's high *C*), striking both notes with the same amount of energy, the higher note will SEEM louder to the listener. Because the human ear is more sensitive to high pitches, particularly in the range of 3,000 hertz, the listener perceives the higher pitch as being louder, even though scientific instruments can demonstrate that the decibel level is exactly the same. (A DECIBEL is a unit used to measure loudness.)

This accounts for the fact that many people turn up the bass on their stereo when they lower the overall volume. Mid- and high-range frequencies can be heard clearly at low-intensity levels; whereas the bass may not be perceived at all if the intensity is below 40 decibels. Consequently, we turn up the bass to balance the mid and high frequencies.

The perception factor of loudness is one which must be taken into consideration by choir directors. Directors must have the basses sing louder on low notes in order to achieve a balance with the high notes of the soprano section, since high pitches are perceived as being louder.

Tone color and emotional intensity also influence the way an audience perceives the loudness of a tone. A more complex harmonic structure is perceived as being louder than one with fewer harmonics, even though the pitch and recorded intensity in decibels are the same. Composers, therefore, write most of the important climaxes of their songs using full instrumentation, high pitches, and high intensities.

HARMONY

When two people harmonize around a piano, they are singing two different notes simultaneously to create a composite, pleasing sound. The

two notes imply a chord (three or more notes played together) which relates
to our concept of how harmony should sound, or of what harmony should
be. Harmony is the putting together of notes which are sung or played simultaneously. Because harmony is what happens along with the melody, it
lends texture, tone color, emotion, energy, and intensity to the melodic line.
It also helps to clarify form.

The history of music—starting in the ninth century—began with a single
melodic line. After several centuries passed, people discovered that more
than one note could be sung or played together and give pleasure to the listener. This was the beginning of harmony.

By the middle of the seventeenth century, harmony had evolved into the
composite sounds which we of the Western world still find pleasing today.
During the fruitful 250-year period between 1650 and 1900, composers
imaginatively created thousands of musical expressions using what actually
is a limited harmonic structure.

In the twentieth century, some composers of contemporary art music
began to expand at an amazing rate the traditional concepts and usage of
harmony. Because our Western ears are still basically accustomed to hearing
the type of harmony used between 1650 and 1900, listeners have had to
make conscious adjustments to the expanded and more flexible concepts of
harmony found in some contemporary music. Most of the music we hear
today (both popular and classical) is still based upon the harmonic structures developed during 250 years preceding 1900.

As a person listens to more of the new music which uses expanded harmonic concepts, he is able to put it together in an order. And, as he becomes
accustomed to this contemporary music, he begins to like it. It no longer
seems unorderly, dissonant, unstructured, unpleasant, and anxiety-provoking
to his Western tradition-oriented ears. Instead, new vistas are opened for the
expression and release of energy and emotion.

Harmony is one of the major elements that create a particular style of
music. As mentioned earlier, most of the music heard today is based upon
the harmony concept of the seventeenth and eighteenth centuries, but within
that concept there are smaller, very structured usages of chordal arrangements and chordal progressions that immediately identify a particular style
of music to our ears. Thus we can perceive immediately whether the musical
style is jazz, country and western, Brahms, Aaron Copland, barbershop, soul,
Wagner, or Bach.

EXERCISE IN SINGING HARMONY

Sing the following song with a friend—one singing the top note (which forms the melody), and the other singing the lower note (the harmony line).

KUM BA YA

Slowly in 3 (♩ = 1 beat)

Nigerian Folk Song

harmony

Kum   Ba   Ya,   my Lord,   Kum   Ba   Ya,___ Kum Ba   Ya,   my Lord,   Kum   Ba

Ya.___ Kum Ba   Ya,   my Lord, Kum   Ba   Ya,___ My   Lord___ Kum Ba   Ya.___

FORM

According to the dictionary, FORM is an arrangement or organization of things to create a coherent image. In music, form refers to the orderly arrangement of smaller parts that creates a complete piece of music. Form is necessary in the simplest of music and in the most complex . . . in a folk song and in a symphony.

The following parts create the form of a musical selection: MOTIF—recurring small patterns, usually two to five notes in each pattern; PHRASE—a melody line that is partially complete, comparable to the phrases in a spoken sentence; MUSICAL SENTENCE—phrases that are put together, similar to a sentence in speech; SECTION—musical sentences that are put together as sentences are put together to make a paragraph; and the WHOLE—sections put together to make a complete piece of music.

Form is one of the major elements in music that keeps the music interesting to the listener. This is accomplished by repeats, contrasts, and balance in melody, rhythm, volume, and tone color, done in an organized fashion.

If the form is not structured, or if it is so complicated that an audience cannot perceive its order, the listeners will become disturbed and anxious. They won't like the music because they will be unable to relate to it as "music"; it will seem more like "noise." When a listener is unable to perceive the structure and order of musical form, he becomes either agitated or bored. (When humans cannot distinguish order, an actual muscle reaction occurs creating tension and fatigue in the body.) However, form can be very disjunctive (as it often is in contemporary art music), but if the audience can mentally order the music—consciously or unconsciously—they will be more inclined to relax and to listen with a more flexible mental attitude.

Most songs have very simple form because songs are usually short and have few sections. Although songs can contain any number of sections, usually they include only two or three. Songs tend to fall into the following types of patterns (each letter refers to one section):

A: A song composed of one section only; called "through-composed." The form of the music follows the form of the text. Examples: "Silent Night," "America the Beautiful," "Erlkönig" by Schubert.

A–B: A song composed of two contrasting sections. Examples: "Pop Goes the Weasel," "Auld Lang Syne."

A–B–A: A three-part song containing an opening section, a contrasting section, and a repeat of the first section. (This is the form used most frequently in songs.) Examples: "Sound of Music," "Camelot," "Caro Mio Ben" by Giordani.

Strophic Song: In this form, several verses of a poem are sung to the same music. Examples: "Abide With Me," "Joy to the World," and most other hymns.

In songs, the form of the poem has considerable effect upon the form of the music. Because phrasing is determined by music and text, singers must make them work together so that the music maintains good form. PHRASING is the separation of the words and music (by a pause or breath) in order to make the song intelligible and give it meaning.

Introduction to Exercises

Form is the combining of elements in some sort of order that has balance. To organize something, to give it general structure, is to give it form. Movement has form; speech has form; every song has form.

In the following exercises you will create form by expressing your own energy in MOVEMENT, SOUND, SPEECH, and SONG. We begin again with energy and progress from movement to sound to speech and then to song because energy sets the stage for the production of song, the final product of our musical instrument.

EXERCISE 1

PURPOSE: Transfer your own energy to movement.
         Create form in movement.

1. Choose an empty, private space where you will not be disturbed in your concentration.
2. Choose two words from the Chart of Energy Types (page 30) that describe ways of releasing energy (vibratory, percussive, staccato, sustained, pendular, lyrical, suspended, collapse).

   A. Transfer your first word choice into movement. Do it WITHOUT music. Use your own energy to express a specific kind of energy in movement. (Example: If you chose the word "percussive," you would make such explosive movements as jabs, punches, slashes, stomps, etc.) While expressing any type of energy, you can stand still and make gestures or you can move around the room. Feel free to do your own expression and remember that you can use:

Various parts of your body	Changes in focus
Changes in direction	Different rhythms
Several levels	Various tempos

   B. Transfer the second word description into movement and this time create movements that offer a contrast to the ones you did with your first word choice. For instance, you might change to lyrical movements that are gliding, flowing, curved, circular, continuous, gentle.

3. Repeat the two types of movements, in sequence, from Section A to B and then back again to A, thus creating a form which is generally called A–B–A.

Congratulations! You have just choreographed a dance sequence. Do not make judgments about whether it is a good or bad dance. Just observe the fact that you have put movements together in a balanced organization called form.

EXERCISE 2

PURPOSE: Transfer your own energy into vocal sounds.
Create form in sound.

1. Add vocal sound to the Section A movements of Exercise 1. The sounds should correspond to the energy of the movements. (If you are making percussive movements, combine percussive sounds with the percussive movements.) Remember that sounds have:

Tone color	Rhythm
Volume	Tempo
Pitch	Line

2. Add vocal sound to the Section B movements. Again, the sounds should correspond to the energy of the movements. (If you are now making lyrical movements, make lyrical sounds.)
3. Put all the sounds and movements together: Section A followed by Section B, and a return to Section A, to create an A–B–A form composed of sound and movement.

EXERCISE 3

PURPOSE: Develop better breath capacity and control.
Establish a cadence.
Compose a melody and a song.

Take a walk around the block, in a park or find a place where you can have privacy.

1. Breath capacity and control
   a. The first part of this exercise uses rhythmical breathing, co-ordinated to your walking rhythm. Be sure to walk in a quick tempo. Sniff in small amounts of air through your nose, puff out gently through the mouth (like blowing out individual candles with your mouth pursed). TAKE *ONE* SNIFF OR PUFF *PER* STEP

    b. Sniff IN 4 times, puff OUT 4 times.   Repeat 4 times.
       Sniff IN 2 times, puff OUT 4 times.   Once only.
       Sniff IN 3 times, puff OUT 1 time.   Once.
       Sniff IN 4 times, puff OUT 8 times.   Once.
       Sniff IN 8 times, puff OUT 8 times.   Once.

    Continue, using any variations of counting that appeal to you.

Should you feel dizzy while doing the breath exercise, do not be alarmed, just sit and rest for a moment. You have sent more oxygen to your brain (a desirable action) than it is normally accustomed to receiving. If you feel dizzy, do the exercise in moderation until you build up greater endurance. Smokers, beware! You will be among those whose lungs need help. Add this exercise to your daily routines and it will improve your state of health!

  2. Start a cadence.
    a. Use any words you wish. Just start saying a cadence while you walk. Say the words in a strong repetitive rhythm. For instance, you might use the phrase "Today Is Tuesday" in the following fashion: (The CAPS indicate a step).

1	2	3	4
step	step	step	step
TO – – – –	DAY	is TUES – –	DAY

    b. Keep the cadence going in a singsong fashion. But change the inflections of your voice.

    c. Allow the inflections of your voice to cover an even WIDER range of pitches.

    d. Try various volumes.

    e. Change the emotion. (Be playful, be determined, be sad.)

    f. Slow down the words, sustaining each word for more than one step. Notice this begins to sound more like singing. That's fine! Let the sound be more like singing and less like speech.

    g. Use more than one pitch per word. Try a musical scale—move the pitch up and down. Co-ordinate or combine words and steps in any way that pleases you.

    h. Say your words three times, using the same inflection (melody) each time. Then invent a new phrase with a new inflection to end

the sequence. This will create a through-composed form consisting
of four balanced phrases.

Today is Tuesday,
Today is Tuesday,
Today is Tuesday,
And I'm going home.

Remember that form is organization, order, pattern. You just created a
song form! Experiment with other forms. Keep repeating your song, using
whatever variations your imagination allows. Expand upon the suggestions and examples presented in this exercise. They are only intended to
help you get started. Have fun!

CHAPTER SIX

THE THREE "E'S" IN SONG

* * *

"TRANSFORMATION"

Something is happening with my singing! I don't sing great yet, but I do sing a lot. And I'm enjoying every minute of it. I'm expressing in ways that I never expressed before. And, you know, it no longer seems to matter as much that I don't sing great. What really matters is that I am singing and it is getting better. A lot better!

The transformation from nonsinger to one who will sing almost at the drop of a hat began way back at that first singing lesson when somehow I found myself making more sounds than I ever thought possible. Later, as the production of sounds came more easily while I practiced in the privacy of my room, I began to feel more secure about my basic ability. I began to think that perhaps there actually was something in that voice box of mine just waiting to be released.

Things really began to happen for me while Joan and I were in the process of selecting and refining the various exercises that we have included in this book. We must have done those exercises a hundred times each. Once I forgot about myself and just concentrated upon doing the exercises, strange things began to happen. I started singing better and enjoying it more. I stopped thinking about "singing." And most important . . . I stopped trying so hard to sing better. I just sang.

One of the exercises held special attraction for me. That's the exercise on page 46 where you read words aloud in response to the energy of a piece of recorded music. I used a microphone, which amplified my normally quiet speaking voice, creating a better balance between music and speech. After

*repeating the exercise many times, using the same music and text, and try-
ing to concentrate on expressing the meaning of the words and the emotion
of the music, it began to sound pretty good!*

*After experimenting further, I found that my speaking voice seemed to
lead right into singing and, before I knew what was happening, I was speaking some parts of the song and singing others . . . doing whichever seemed
to be called for in the music. It was great fun! What really surprised me,
though, was that the more I concentrated upon expressing the emotion of
the song and the more I stopped thinking about my poor singing, the better
the singing became!*

*Talk about miracles! That exercise gave birth to a singer. An infant singer,
to be sure. But a singer, nonetheless.*

RICKY

LEARNING TO SING SONGS

When a person decides to learn a new skill, he can approach it in one of
two ways. He can either take the gestalt approach and attempt to grasp the
entire skill all at once OR he can pursue it in bits and pieces and learn each
part of the entire skill in a systematic fashion. Both of these approaches are
valuable in learning to sing, but since we have already established a founda-
tion in previous exercises, we will concentrate in this chapter upon the gestalt
approach. (Exercises to build specific vocal skills will be presented in Chapter
Eight.)

The act of singing might be construed as somewhat intimidating if we
paused to consider that singing is a vocal expression, a musical expression, a
language expression, a physical feeling in the vocal instrument, an outer
visual expression of body language, and an expression of the singer's inner
emotional feeling about the song. Whew! That seems like an extraordinary
task! But humans are extraordinary creatures, so much so that we can combine all of the above without a moment's hesitation. In fact, we do it all the
time in speech, and we can do the very same thing in singing.

When we were young children just learning to speak, we didn't analyze
or pay attention to the details of language. We observed our parents, listened
to them, imitated them, and we spoke! We were probably somewhat blasé
about doing it too, even though our parents may have been so excited that
they recorded our initial utterances for posterity.

In the speech learning process, we discovered that the reproduction of certain language sounds was more difficult than others and took us longer to accomplish (remember the "th" and "r" sounds?). But we kept on listening, imitating, comparing our speech to others, practicing and learning. We learned the total product of speech without being concerned about grammar, phonetics, or acoustics. We simply talked. And now that we are adults, even though we may not speak perfectly on all counts, we do speak very well indeed. We function quite adequately in society, and that is an extraordinary accomplishment!

We can learn to sing by following exactly the same procedure used in learning to speak: by listening, concentrating, imitating, comparing, practicing, and accomplishing. We might even discover that the initial results of this process are spectacular! It is very likely that we would sing with beauty, security, and rich emotional expression IF we were able to:

1. Free ourselves from self-criticism, self-doubt and general mental and physical tensions.
2. Listen carefully to other singers and then imitate our model-singers calmly and attentively.
3. Allow ourselves to feel, absorb, and express the energy and emotion of the music.

REMEMBER: Our body already knows how to sing IF we will only allow it to sing.

The greatest hurdle that an adult must overcome in learning to sing is to free himself from SELF-DOUBT and SELF-CRITICISM. Those of us who want to improve our singing must stop doubting and criticizing ourselves. We must allow ourselves to "let go" . . . relax . . . stop worrying!

Successful singing occurs when we are able to sing without confusing our self-worth with our singing. It is imperative not to equate success or failure in the performance of a song with our success or failure as a person. Like oil and water . . . these two elements just don't mix!

To sing a song successfully via the gestalt approach requires the ability to concentrate upon and then express the ESSENCE of the song. (The "essence" of a song refers to its energy, to the message of its lyrics, and to its emotion—the humor, passion, joy, exultation, or sadness of the words and music.)

Now that you have performed the fundamental exercises presented thus far and have gained a better understanding of the close relationship between speech and singing, we will ask you to perform two additional exercises. The first is a preparatory exercise in *concentration* in which you will focus upon expressing the essence of a song in your *imagination*. In the second exercise, you will transfer your powers of concentration into actually *singing a song*.

CONCENTRATION

The upcoming exercise in concentration involves selecting a recorded song that appeals to you . . . one that you relate to emotionally and intellectually and which is reasonably compatible with your present musical and vocal skills. Then you will listen to the recording while feeling comfortable and relaxed. Allow yourself to be at ease in body and mind, and direct your attention to the energy of the melody and words, to the emotion of the music. Enjoy the music. Become familiar with the music, allowing the learning to happen naturally and easily. Don't try to force it. Just let the learning happen.

Next, you will IMAGINE yourself singing by picturing yourself in your mind's eye standing, singing, feeling confident and free of worry and concern. Your shoulders, neck, face will feel at ease, free of tension. The movements of your body will respond naturally to the energy of the music. Your imagined vocal sounds will be expressive because your psyche focuses upon the music, its energy, emotion, and message. You sing beautifully, expressively, confidently . . . in your imagination.

As soon as you can imagine feeling confident and free of worry and nervousness, and as soon as you feel comfortable with the melody and words and can "hear" them in your mind, then you will focus all of your concentration into expressing, in your imagined singing, the essence of the song.

Anytime that your CONCENTRATION is absolutely focused upon the music and the message of the song—and not upon yourself—you will convey the essence of the song. When you think about the song only, and not about how well or poorly you are singing it, you will know that it is "right." Remember that old saying: "When you fall in love, you will know it!" Likewise, when you achieve absolute, total concentration on a song, it will feel *right* and you'll *know* it! Whether your singing is imagined or real.

What if your fears about singing are so great that you can't even imagine yourself singing without fear? If you experience this degree of apprehension about singing, even when singing in the quiet of your mind, then repeat the exercise in stages. If at any step you become nervous, anxious, apprehensive, or if any of your muscles tighten . . . STOP RIGHT THERE. Repeat the previous steps until you feel ready to take the successive step in your imagination feeling easy, calm, and free. When you are able to imagine the entire process with confidence, you are ready to go to the next step of singing aloud. If you feel that your concentration is less than it should be, keep on trying. The art of concentration is learned and improves with practice.

EXERCISE 1

PURPOSE: To enhance powers of concentration and imagination.

1. Select and play a piece of music that you really like.
2. Sit down or lie on your back in a comfortable environment.
3. Listen to the music, allowing yourself to "feel" the music, responding to its rhythm, tempo, and intensity.
4. Listen to the melody and words until you are familiar with them.
5. In your thoughts, begin to move to the music, using small or large movements. Move a finger or your whole body. Build upon your body movements until you are standing and moving in place or across the room, wherever the music leads you. REMEMBER: THIS IS ALL TAKING PLACE IN YOUR IMAGINATION ONLY! DO NOT ACTUALLY STAND OR MOVE.
6. Begin to sing the song (in your imagination). Sing softly at first, then louder.
7. Imagine singing to a trusted friend.
8. Imagine standing on a stage.
9. Imagine singing to your friend from the stage.
10. Imagine singing to an audience that cheers your performance.

SINGING A SONG

Now that you have experienced in your imagination the freedom, expression, and pleasure of successful singing, transfer the IMAGINED experience into a REAL one. Sing a song . . . right now! Follow the same steps that you used in your imagined singing experience—at least through the step where you sing for yourself alone in the comfort and privacy of your room. If you feel ready to sing for others, do that too. You are completely in charge. Do what YOU want to do. Sing! Here's how:

EXERCISE 2

PURPOSE: To learn and sing a song.

1. Select a recorded song which you enjoy listening to . . . one that you can
   identify with and which is compatible with your present musical and vocal
   skills. (It is a good idea to select the same song used in the previous
   exercise.)
2. Then listen to the recording and enjoy the music. Remain comfortable
   and relaxed.
3. Begin to "feel" the music, responding to its rhythm, tempo, intensity, energy, and emotion.
4. Listen to the melody and words until you are familiar with them. Don't
   become intent upon trying to learn the melody and words. Just let the
   learning happen while you are enjoying the music.
5. Stand up and begin to move to the music, feeling free and easy, secure
   and confident, your movement directed by the energy of the music.
6. IMAGINE yourself singing the song beautifully, expressively, confidently.
7. Now, actually begin to SING the song ALOUD, using the singer on the
   recording as a guide. Imitate the way your model-singer performs the
   song. Think about the song, not about how you are singing it. Concentrate and focus upon expressing the energy and emotion of the song.
8. Enjoy the music, the song, and the singing of the song. Enjoy the freedom
   and pleasure of expressing in words and music the energy and emotion of
   the song. That's what singing is all about . . . *energy, emotion, expression!*

Congratulations . . . you have sung a SONG!!! Sing it again and again
and again. The singing and the expression get easier and better every time
you do it. Keep in mind that gymnasts, pianists, public speakers, etc., do not
achieve perfection the first time, nor the first several times, they try. They
work up to their potential. Singers work up to their potential too.

I realize that it is human nature to evaluate our own performance, as well
as that of others. So I expect that you will evaluate your singing, but I hope
that you don't criticize it. Evaluation is healthy, but criticism is destructive!
And, please, try to keep your evaluation in perspective. If you found that
you had some trouble "carrying the tune," don't shrug your shoulders in dis-

gust and decide that you're not a singer. Don't say: "I'm no good!" It simply isn't true. If you had difficulty hearing or reproducing pitches, it just means you had difficulty hearing or reproducing pitches. That is part of the learning process and you can improve it. (Refer back to Chapter Four for help with pitch problems.)

Perhaps you found that although you were able to capture and express the emotion and message of the song, there were also some incorrect pitches and you lost the melody for a while. This doesn't indicate that you can't learn music or that you can never be a good musician. All it means is that you need to keep on trying until you become more familiar with the melody.

Return to your model-singer, listen to the way he sings the song, sing along with him in your mind, and then sing out loud. As long as you permit the learning to "happen," without trying too hard or becoming tense about "making" the pitches correct, your pitch memory and reproduction will improve steadily.

A few wrong pitches won't ruin a song. Even professional singers hit wrong pitches occasionally. (Including me. That's one reason I practice a lot!) Getting the melody absolutely right may require many sessions of listening, imagining doing it correctly, and then doing it correctly. Keep on trying and trusting. The accuracy of melody will improve as long as you don't become bogged down in worrying about it. Relax and allow the learning process to be a pleasurable one.

No one should depreciate his voice because:

The smallest voice can have carrying power.
The breathiest voice can gain clarity and authority.
The short-breathed singer can gain breath control.
The strident voice can gain mellowness, sweetness, beauty.
The nasal voice can gain sonority.

A beginning singer should approach singing with the realization that his voice is already perfect. In other words, he already has at his command everything he needs to make music. When he eliminates the inefficient, constricting habits and attitudes that restrict him from producing easy, sustained musical sounds, his TRUE VOICE will emerge. When a singer discovers his true voice, it will *feel* and *sound* good!

If you don't like the way your voice sounds now, remember that the vocal instrument can make an astonishing number of different sounds (qualities). Again, it is a matter of listening to someone whose vocal quality you like, imagining yourself producing the same quality that he does, and then comparing and trying until you succeed in producing it too. It may be helpful in this situation to watch how your model-singer produces his vocal quality. Tune in and observe him the next time he appears on television.

If you find that you can imagine a desired vocal quality in your mind, which continues to be considerably different from the sound you produce and you continue to have interfering tensions, you might consider going to a voice teacher for some help. Also, it may be helpful to refer back to Chapter Four and the section on Tone Color, p. 56.

If you will trust your body to respond to your mental image of a song and if you will free yourself to follow the suggestions we have given you, you WILL be able to make many beneficial adjustments in your singing. You will be able to sing and enjoy doing it. Once again, the steps to the ANYONE CAN SING method are:

1. **LISTEN** to the music carefully but without tension.
2. Pick a **MODEL-SINGER** who falls within the range of your current musical and vocal skills. (Don't choose Roberta Peters singing the "Queen of the Night" aria from *The Magic Flute,* requiring a high *F* above high *C,* if you have a 1½-octave range. If you have a soft, muted voice, don't choose Aretha Franklin for your model. Choose a model-singer of your same sex. Be reasonable. You can challenge yourself later!)
3. **FEEL** the music, allowing it to energize your body and stimulate your emotions and your desire to make a physical and vocal expression.
4. **IMAGINE** yourself singing like your model.
5. **CONCENTRATE** upon the music, not upon yourself.
6. **SING** the song, imitating your model.
7. **THINK** about expressing the song, not about how you are singing it.
8. **TRUST** your body to do what you have imagined it doing.
9. **ENJOY** the freedom and pleasure and expression of singing.
10. **CONTINUE** to repeat these steps until you accomplish what you want to do.

As you repeat the ANYONE CAN SING method over an extended period of time, your body will begin to take over and produce what you desire. Trust your body and don't try to force it. With practice, your body will co-ordinate properly and your singing will show consistent improvement. After you have learned one song, use the same method to learn another song . . . and another . . . and another!

Remember that the major obstacle most people encounter in singing is not their vocal instrument or musical shortcomings or physical disabilities. It is their EMOTIONAL STATE OF MIND, the tensions, constrictions, fears, inhibitions, anxieties, hang-ups, shyness, feelings of inadequacy, the misconceptions about learning attitudes, and all the assorted factors that contribute to one's image of self. When the interfering obstacles are dealt with and eliminated, the voice is there . . . ready to function, ready to SING BEAUTIFULLY!

CHAPTER SEVEN

A SINGER'S GUIDE

* * *

SIMPLY SINGING

Now that you are among those who do sing and now that you have discovered that by singing more you will sing better and with greater enjoyment, it might be helpful to consider the various outlets available for singing socially and some of the other learning alternatives about singing that are open to you.

A great many people are content to sing simply for their own personal enjoyment, for the pleasure and cathartic release of singing. These are the people who sing brief snatches of songs when they are at home alone or while driving in their car. Sometimes they sing along to music played on TV, radio, or the stereo. They enjoy singing, feel comfortable enough with their singing ability to sing whenever they feel like it, and don't necessarily feel the need or the motivation to make singing a more active part of their lives.

If you fit into this category of singers . . . fine! Continue to sing whenever the spirit moves you to sing. You have probably already discovered that the more you sing, the better you sing. Feel free to sing, have fun singing, and do it often. You might also enjoy a new experience of singing along to special instrumental recordings that are now available to provide musical accompaniment for singers (and for other instruments as well). Such recordings are produced by Music Minus One (43 West Sixty-first Street, New York, N.Y. 10023) and Educo Records (P.O. Box 3006, Ventura, California 93003). They may be ordered directly or through catalogs available at the larger music stores.

But don't forget that there is another opportunity available to novice singers—the pleasure and fellowship of singing with others. Seek out a group of friends who also like to sing and sing together around a piano, with guitar accompaniment, or to favorite records. Have a jam session or sing-along party. Sing with your family.

You might also consider joining a choir, chorus, or barbershop organization such as SPEBSQSA (for men) or Harmony, Inc. (for women). Almost every community offers organized group activities for singers of all ages and stages of proficiency, including church, civic, and university groups. Some of the larger organizations may require auditions, but many others accept all applicants.

If you are uncertain about what organized singing activities are available in your community, check with your friends or with any choir director (from church, school, etc.). You might also call the local Chamber of Commerce or your community Parks and Recreation Department for information concerning choir organizations. Tell them that you like to sing; advise whether or not you read music and whether you have previous experience singing with a choir. Then ask if they know of a group that meets your specific requirements.

Joining any choral organization involves a certain commitment to the group because it will require at least one rehearsal each week. It doesn't take long, though, before every choir member discovers a keen sense of personal satisfaction in being part of a "team," particularly as a new song is learned and gradually evolves into a beautiful musical expression of the group. How very different a choral number sounds in performance compared to the way it sounded during the first rehearsal!

CHOIR AND SOLO SINGING

Many singers derive considerable rewards from becoming actively involved in their choral group activities. However, to become a strongly contributing member of any choral group requires at least four basic musical skills. They are:

1. The ability to read music (sight-read),
2. The ability to use the voice well enough to sing pitches with good intonation (to reproduce extremely accurate and well-tuned pitches),
3. The ability to blend with the group (to use a voice quality that matches the needs of the group), and
4. Sufficient breath control.

A person can teach himself to read music if he has the discipline and patience to take the time and effort to do it. A number of good "how to" books are available, including: *Henscratches and Flyspecks* by Pete Seeger (Berkley Medallion Books); *Learn To Read Music* by Howard Shanet (Simon & Schuster); and *Rudiments of Music* by Robert W. Ottman and Frank Mainous (Prentice-Hall).

Although there are some choir directors who assist their members in learning to read music, perhaps the most efficient method is to seek professional help from a voice or piano teacher. Another approach is to contact the music theory teacher at your local university and tell him that you are interested in learning to read music and sight-read. He may then be able to recommend a competent student to tutor you for a few private sessions.

If you are having difficulties with intonation, tonal quality, or breath control, some of the exercises in the next chapter may be helpful. These exercises are limited, of course, since singing is an oral expression and the correction of vocal problems often requires professional guidance from a qualified teacher who can provide the necessary demonstration, feedback, and appropriate technical suggestions. Therefore, if you are unable to correct your problems by yourself, don't hesitate to seek help from the choir director or to ask his advice about where to get professional help from another source.

It is possible for a person to sing quite attractively without ever reaching his maximum potential, without learning to use his voice most efficiently. Such singers can be strong choir members. But if your personal goal is to improve sufficiently to become a soloist, or if you want to improve your vocal technique as a soloist, I suggest you give careful consideration to studying voice with a competent professional.

A good vocal technique is one that has ease of production and control of tonal quality and of long, sustained tones, achieving a maximum result with a minimum amount of effort. A good vocal technique, then, is one that is both HEALTHY and EFFICIENT.

For a singer to reach a high level of his singing potential requires that he develop a good vocal technique and improved musical and expressive skills. There exists a vast body of knowledge about the art of singing, and an informed voice teacher, who is sympathetic with your personal singing goals, is the person to turn to for help to uncover this knowledge, to incorporate it into your singing, and to increase your proficiency as an expressive performer.

STUDYING SINGING

A student of voice is any person who takes professional instruction because he wants to change existing inefficient vocal habits and learn to sing better. How long the learning process will take depends upon the student's personal goal in singing—whether he just wants to sing better or to learn to sing his best—and it depends upon the present state of his technique and singing ability.

The process begins with finding the right teacher to meet the student's needs. Therefore, the student must first clearly understand his own goals and decide whether he wants to spend the money on lessons and devote the required number of hours to practice. If his desire to improve his singing is strong enough to spend valuable time and money on lessons and practice, then he must also decide whether his goal is to improve his abilities in order to sing solos with groups, necessitating improved vocal skills and performing abilities; or whether he wants to become a serious student of voice because of the profound challenge and pleasure of singing; whether he desires to sing a single style of music or a variety of styles; or whether his goal is to eventually become a professional singer (to make his living from singing—as an opera singer, gospel singer, popular singer, country and western singer, jazz singer, paid choir singer, etc.).

These decisions will directly affect the type or types of professional he studies with because, depending upon the student's goals, he can choose from a wide selection of professional people who work with singers. Among the various types of professionals are:

1. The VOICE TEACHER—who trains the vocal instrument, teaches music and songs and their interpretation, trains the entire person for performance and offers an environment where the student may perform for his fellow students.

2. The VOCAL COACH—usually a pianist or conductor, who trains singers in musical style and interpretation. Some vocal coaches have a broad vocal knowledge and some do not.

3. The MUSIC TEACHER—who teaches basic music reading and music principles, usually on an instrument other than the voice (such as piano).

4. The COACH / ACCOMPANIST—who teaches the correct reading of a song (to reproduce the music accurately) and accompanies the singer in rehearsal and performance.

5. The COACH / STYLIST—who works with specific styles of music, such as jazz or French art songs.

6. The ACCOMPANIST—who plays the piano accompaniment for lessons or performance.

7. The CHOIR DIRECTOR—who organizes and leads the choir, working primarily with choral music and choral ensemble sound. (Although choir directors usually have a good vocal knowledge, there are some whose only background is in piano and organ and who know surprisingly little about the vocal instrument.)

8. The ARRANGER—who makes musical arrangements of songs to meet specific needs such as the correct key for a singer, a special style or instrumentation.

9. The COMPOSER—who writes music.

10. The COMPOSITION TEACHER—who teaches basic principles of music, composition, and arranging.

11. The MUSIC THEORY TEACHER—who teaches basic principles of music.

12. The SPEECH TEACHER / VOCAL COACH—who works with the speaking voice.

13. The DRAMA COACH—who works with interpretation and characterization for the theater, musical comedy, opera, TV, etc.

14. The DANCE TEACHER—who works with body movement and dance.

15. The CHOREOGRAPHER—who designs and creates movements and dances for specific performances.

16. The AGENT—who works for the professional singer to book jobs and charges a percentage of the performance fee.

17. The PERSONAL MANAGER—who represents the singer and directs his career, usually earning a set fee or a percentage of the income.

18. The PERSONAL REPRESENTATIVE—who gets bookings and manages the publicity for the singer, usually earning a set fee and/or a percentage.

Most beginning students will find that working with a good voice teacher —either in a private lesson or group session—is the best way to begin vocal studies. Some voice teachers teach privately in the community; others are associated with larger organizations such as junior colleges and universities. Studying voice at a university offers an advantage in that it entitles the student to use a practice room with a piano. This can be a significant factor for people who live in apartments and have trouble finding a suitably private place to practice. Another alternative is to investigate large music and piano stores. Sometimes they rent practice rooms at the store or have pianos available for the student to rent for use at his residence. Every serious voice student should own a piano, stereo, cassette, tape deck, and (if he is primarily interested in popular singing) an amplification system with microphones.

Basic to finding the right voice teacher for you is having a clear understanding of the areas in which a good voice teacher must be competent. To begin with, the teacher must be knowledgeable in the field of VOICE SCIENCE, including:

1. The anatomy and physiology of the larynx, respiratory system, and vocal tract;
2. The acoustic characteristics of speech and the International Phonetic Alphabet (IPA);
3. The relationship of physiology and acoustics to vocal function, which determines the best use of the vocal instrument; and
4. A structured method of exercises for achieving best vocal use.

In addition, the teacher must be thoroughly versed in the field of MUSIC, including:

1. The history, structure, and styles of music;
2. Vocal literature (a wide variety of solo and ensemble literature);
3. Piano skills for accompaniment; and
4. Vocal skills for demonstration.

Thirdly, a good voice teacher will be skilled in:

1. Developing CREATIVITY in the areas of music, movement, interpretation, drama, and poetry;
2. LANGUAGES (English and foreign languages);
3. BEHAVIORAL SCIENCE; and
4. Various PEDAGOGICAL METHODS.

Last, and equally important, a good voice teacher will have PERSONAL QUALITIES that combine a genuine respect and fondness for the students with a deep love of music. A good teacher maintains a lifelong personal in-

trospection and flexibility in order that a productive interpersonal relationship and communication with the students will flourish and grow.

Finding a voice teacher is not difficult, but finding a good one is quite a
different matter because the quality of instruction varies widely. Unlike
some professions, there is no accrediting agency for voice teaching. Therefore, it is imperative that the prospective student be able to distinguish between poor, adequate, and excellent teaching.

The way to begin acquiring names of voice teachers is to ask around. If
you know student singers whose singing appeals to you, inquire who their
teachers are. If you encounter good professional singers, ask with whom
they have studied. Check with a choir director (of civic groups, churches,
public or private schools) for recommendations. Call the music department
at your local junior college or university. Check with professional organizations such as the National Association of Teachers of Singing, the Music
Teachers National Association, and the Federation of Music Clubs. Members
of these organizations will be in touch with the prominent professionals in
your community.

Once you obtain a list of names of professional voice teachers, begin to investigate them personally. Remember that having a university degree in
voice does not always guarantee that the teacher will do his job well, and
that very often good performers are poor teachers. But don't be discouraged.
There are many fine voice teachers, and if you persevere you will find the
best one for you.

How do you decide who IS a good teacher? I think one of the best ways to
begin is to ask a prospective teacher if you can listen to his students in performance. Then observe whether the students sing easily and pleasurably, if
they have a natural involvement with the music (as opposed to being rigid
or sterile), and if they seem to use their voices healthfully and efficiently.

If you like what you see and hear in performance, ask the teacher for an
interview. Ask about his goals in teaching; tell him your goals in voice
study; and determine whether they synchronize philosophically, musically,
and in terms of your long-range plans. Since you will work very closely with
your voice teacher and will be seeing him regularly, be certain that you like
and respect him and that you feel you can work comfortably with him.

Once you find a teacher who meets these criteria, take a few lessons from
him. If you don't relate well together, consider changing teachers. (But
don't change just because miracles didn't happen overnight. Vocal improvement takes time, practice, and determination!) After you locate a teacher
with whom you feel comfortable, plan to study with him for the duration of
your training period (from two to six years, with four years as a reasonable

average). Should you decide to become a professional singer, your vocal studies will continue for a lifetime. There are also many people who continue to study after having reached a high level of proficiency simply because of the pleasure of the lesson, which at this stage of advancement becomes a musical rehearsal.

SINGING LESSONS

Voice lessons are offered in private sessions which last for a half hour or an hour, and are usually taken once or twice a week. The cost varies between $8 and $25 an hour ($4 to $12.50 a half hour). Some teachers, who work primarily with professional singers, charge up to $50 an hour. The cost of the lesson does not always correlate with the quality of instruction. Sometimes it merely reflects geographic location or what the traffic will bear!

Lessons may also be taken in small group situations called voice classes. This is often an excellent arrangement for the beginning student because it enables him to learn basic vocal technique from a professional teacher at a lower cost, usually between $4 and $6 for a one-hour weekly session. Recommended class size is between six and ten people. Students normally sign up for a course lasting anywhere from four months to one year. Very often these classes are offered at colleges as extension courses.

I recommend group classes for the first year of study because, besides being less expensive, small group sessions offer the advantage of superior auditory training. In addition to hearing the teacher, the student has an opportunity to hear other singers at a level of vocal advancement similar to his own. Also, it very often happens that a pleasant group spirit develops among the students, since they are all working toward a common goal. Group sessions also provide a place to learn to perform before an audience without anxiety.

There is a drawback to class study in that a one-hour session does not permit enough time for each student to perform a sufficient number of songs. Therefore, I suggest either that the sessions be two hours long (for six to ten students), or that students supplement their one-hour class sessions with additional private lessons taken weekly or twice a month.

As studies progress, private voice lessons become increasingly important because of the growing need for individual instruction, faster progress, expanded literature, and the development of performance skills.

Basically, the study of voice includes:

1. Learning the auditory discrimination of tonal qualities in order to establish the parameters of vocal production.

2. Understanding the vocal instrument and acquiring technical vocal skills. (Through the use of imagery, physical directions, and musical suggestions, the teacher guides the student in learning new physical responses and the production of free, easy, appropriate, healthy, and effective tonal qualities. In this way, the student gains vocal control and an expressive use of his voice.)

3. Learning music principles, including how to learn music accurately from a written score, how to interpret the intentions of the composer, how to create a musical style.

4. Learning a variety of songs to build an expanded repertoire.

5. Developing successful, creative, expressive, artistic performing skills.

The above five items are basic to voice study, but there are other peripheral benefits inherent in each voice lesson. Because a student charges his vocal teacher with the responsibility of changing a part of himself, the teacher becomes a trusted friend who helps the student to gain self-confidence and grow in his love of music and singing, encourages experimentation without criticism, guides in the development of appropriate judgment, and renders advice about perseverance, professionalism, musical curiosity, and self-discipline . . . all of which are vital ingredients in performance.

It occurs to me that some readers may be astonished at the number of years that serious students must devote to the study of voice in order to achieve a high level of proficiency. But when you consider that the study of singing requires the changing of basic human behavioral habits that are an integral part of the student's personality, perhaps it becomes easier to comprehend.

Not only does the student singer learn a healthy and efficient use of the vocal mechanism, he must also change any habitual behavior patterns that interfere with effective singing. These automatic habits are so deeply a part of our self-concept that to even become aware of them, let alone change them, is time-consuming.

In addition, a student singer deals with a complex vocal apparatus and mechanism which requires the skillful, knowledgeable use of muscles and organs that are not directly observable or even under his direct control. Because singing is an oral/aural art, it requires extensive training to learn to hear subtle differences between tonal qualities and to relate the difference to the function of the vocal mechanism.

Learning to sing to the best of one's ability is a complex learning process that places great demands on the student's dedication and determination. Yet, without a doubt, it is one of the most satisfying and thrilling of all human endeavors!

CHAPTER EIGHT

TRAINING THE INSTRUMENT

TRAINING THE INSTRUMENT

A voice student acquires technical vocal skills in two ways: He studies the FUNCTION of his instrument ("how" and "why" it works as it does) and he practices a PROGRAMMED SERIES OF SKILL-BUILDING EXERCISES that are carefully designed (by his teacher) to promote a healthy and efficient use of the voice.

Think back for a moment to the vocal exercises that concluded Chapter One. Although the exercises may have appeared to be generalized, actually they were constructed very carefully to help novice singers begin to improve the use of their voice. For example, by singing softly on easy pitches the singer initiated sound without pressure and constriction, thus beginning to learn better breath-larynx co-ordination. In addition, he was asked to sustain his tones, thereby breathing in the easy, comfortable, rhythmical fashion suitable for singing.

When he changed from vowel to vowel, he initiated the process of discrimination in the areas of diction and resonance. By singing "Row Your Boat" both more softly and higher, he began to sing higher pitches with less breath pressure and perhaps even began to sing "on the breath" (floating the tones), thus gaining correct phonic breath support and good vocal "attack." When he tapped his imagination and sang the song in response to different mental images, he stimulated his musical creativity and expression.

There are an almost unlimited number of vocal exercises in existence, most of which require the guidance of a teacher to insure that they are performed properly. However, there are many other exercises, such as the ones presented throughout this book, that a student can perform safely on his own and that may help to correct certain problem areas if they are performed *correctly* and *faithfully*.

The remainder of this chapter is devoted to various kinds of exercises used by serious students of voice in developing technical skills. They are basic exercises, but they do *not* comprise a complete course in vocal study. (A complete study program would fill an entire book in itself and necessitates the guidance and assistance of a teacher.) However, if you will practice the exercises contained in ANYONE CAN SING, in the prescribed manner, there should be noticeable improvement in your singing. Experiment with your voice and enjoy investigating its potential!

Some of the forthcoming exercises are instructional (to help you discover desirable responses). Once a desirable response is acquired, it is not necessary to repeat the exercise. The remaining exercises (those that are identified by a star) should be incorporated into daily *warm-up* sessions. A warm-up session is a time to physically prepare yourself to sing songs. Each warm-up session should begin with the "Ohm" chants (see Chapter One) and include one or more exercises from each of the following categories:

1. Movement exercises (Chapter Two)
2. Breath exercises (Chapter Eight—starred)
3. Attack, Voicing, Registration, Vertical Larynx Position exercises (Chapter Eight—starred)
4. Vowel exercises (Chapter Eight—starred)
5. Articulation exercises (Chapter Eight—starred)

It is not necessary to practice all of the starred exercises every day, but they should all be practiced within a week's time. Periodically, you may find it helpful to tape-record your practice sessions to better evaluate your progress.

The goal of vocal exercises is to enable you to sing songs better. If you practice thirty minutes a day, five days a week (warming-up for fifteen minutes and singing songs for fifteen minutes), you should develop sufficient security and control to make noticeable vocal improvement and to derive more and more pleasure from singing.

The basic skill-building exercises are divided into sections on:

1. Relaxation (beginning on page 127)
2. Posture (page 129)
3. Breath (page 129)

I. Relaxation

The exercises presented in this section are designed to help you discover whether you have hypertension in your sound-producing mechanism or in other parts of your body and, if you do, to help you eliminate the tension. It is necessary to consider the entire body, because hypertension in *any part of the body* directly contributes to constriction in the throat.

EXERCISE 1: BODY RELAXATION

PURPOSE: To contrast the difference between hypertension and relaxation.
To eliminate hypertension throughout the body.

a. Lie down on a bed or on the floor. Consciously relax body tension by speaking silently to each part of your body. Tell your legs, back, arms, shoulders, neck, jaw, eyes, face, etc. to relax . . . to become lax. Tell yourself to sink into the bed or floor, allowing it to support your weight. Have another person move a part of your body in order to check whether it is relaxed. There should be no resistance when someone moves part of your body.

b. Now reverse the procedure. Tighten your body as rigidly as you can. Make your shoulders, back, neck, face, etc. hypertense. Hold for several seconds.

c. Then relax completely, feeling even more relaxed than before. Notice the contrast between total relaxation and hypertension.

✳ EXERCISE 2: RAG DOLL

PURPOSE: To discover body relaxation.

a. Stand up, keeping in mind the kinesthetic sensation of relaxation experienced in the previous exercise. Bend your knees slightly, moving
   the knees outward at a 45-degree angle. Bend over from the hips,
   rounding the back, until your head hangs between the knees. Be as
   flexible as a rag doll. Check your neck to be sure that it is relaxed
   and hanging freely. If someone pushes down gently on your back,
   you are so loose that you bounce up and down easily.

b. Stand up slowly and straighten your back until you achieve an erect,
   balanced posture while maintaining the same lack of muscle tension
   you experienced in your back and neck in the rag-doll position.

   Your head is the last part of your body to straighten up. Feel it
   balance upon your shoulders. Your face should feel relaxed, your
   expression open, and your eyes bright.

c. Repeat several times.

EXERCISE 3: BODY FREEDOM

PURPOSE: To maintain body relaxation while sitting and standing.

a. Stand up and inhale deeply, then exhale slowly. Three times. Maintain the feeling of body balance and lack of hypertension that was
   discovered in the rag-doll position.

b. Sit tall on a chair, in an alert posture with your head balanced upon
   your shoulders. Inhale deeply and exhale slowly. Three times. Maintain body balance and freedom from hypertension (in the back,
   shoulders, and neck).

c. Sigh, first while sitting and then standing. Allow the chest to relax
   during each sigh and notice the freedom of a relaxed throat. It should
   feel very comfortable and relaxed. Repeat three times.

II. Posture

Posture has a direct influence upon the entire sound-producing mechanism because a good, balanced posture (without being rigid) is the first essential in establishing the best use of breath for singing. A balanced posture is one that is alert and comfortably erect without being too rigid or formal. A stance that is sloppy or too casual results in a loss of breath capacity, control and efficiency; too rigid a stance produces hypertension, the archenemy of every singer. Maintaining a smooth, steady, controlled flow of air lies at the very heart of good singing. But the only way this can happen is if the posture permits it to happen!

EXERCISE 4: POSTURE

PURPOSE: To experience a balanced, erect posture.

    a. Stand against a wall, with your heels, buttocks, upper back, shoulders, and head touching the wall. If you find it difficult or uncomfortable to place your head against the wall, it is probably because you are stooping your shoulders and collapsing your chest. Straighten your shoulders, but remember that a taut, rigid military stance is as undesirable in singing as a slouch. Imagine that there are strings attached to the top of both ears, pulling upward. Be sure the strings are attached to the ears, NOT to the nose!

    b. Walk away from the wall, maintaining the same posture. You should feel alert and erect, but not tense or rigid.

III. Breath

A good inhalation for singing involves two major movements 1) The contraction and lowering of the diaphragm into the abdominal area (causing an outward movement in the upper abdomen) and 2) an outward and upward movement of the rib cage. (Refer to inhalation diagram.)

The following breath exercises are designed to help you discover the musculature involved in singing and to build toward the development of increased breath capacity and breath control. As is true of all vocal exercises, breath exercises are not intended just to promote intellectual and physical awareness (although such awareness is helpful); they are designed to establish *good singing habits*. Therefore, they must be performed faithfully, on a daily basis, for as long as it takes to change old habits into new ones. Even then, some of these exercises will be maintained in the singer's exercise repertoire for use in his warm-up sessions. Every singer recognizes that it is as important for a singer to warm-up properly before performance as it is for an athlete.

NOTE: All breath exercises should first be performed while lying on your back on the floor, with your legs straight out on the floor and your arms resting easily at your sides. When you are confident that you are doing an exercise correctly, then try it while standing erect and maintaining the same procedures used on the floor. Always be sure to keep a comfortably alert posture and to inhale comfortably and deeply, using rib and diaphragm movement.

EXERCISE 5: POSTURE AND BREATH

PURPOSE: To discover a good inhalation method for singing.

Lie on the floor on your back, with your legs straight out on the floor and your arms resting easily at your sides. This is the same posture position used in the previous exercise when you stood against the wall. Relax your shoulders against the floor.

a. *Diaphragm breathing:* Place your hands on your stomach at the waistline. Breathe in and feel the in-and-out movement at the waist. This movement occurs when the diaphragm is used during inhalation and actually lowers into the abdominal area. Keep the ribs still in this portion of the exercise.

b. *Rib Breathing:* Place your hands on your sides on the lower ribs. Inhale by lifting *only* the rib cage. Keep the abdomen and diaphragm relaxed. The waist will flatten during rib breathing because the abdomen is sucked inward as the relaxed diaphragm is pulled upward.

c. *Diaphragm-rib Breathing:* Neither of the above methods of inhalation is sufficient to produce efficient singing, because maximum breath capacity requires that *both movements occur simultaneously*. Therefore, in this portion of the exercise, experiment with trying to do both movements at the same time . . . trying to inhale so that the dia-

INHALATION

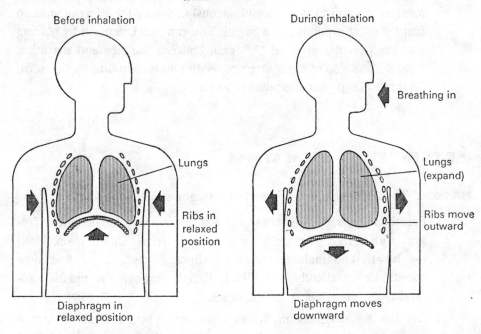

Before inhalation

During inhalation

Lungs

Lungs (expand)

Ribs in relaxed position

Ribs move outward

Breathing in

Diaphragm in relaxed position

Diaphragm moves downward

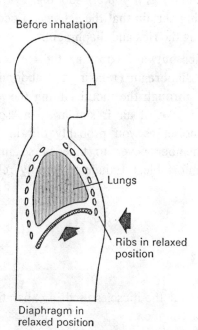

Before inhalation

Lungs

Ribs in relaxed position

Diaphragm in relaxed position

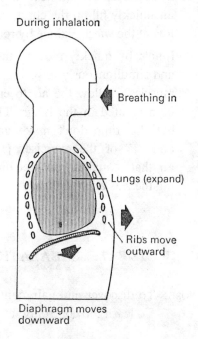

During inhalation

Breathing in

Lungs (expand)

Ribs move outward

Diaphragm moves downward

phragm moves downward toward the feet (causing an outward movement at the waist) while simultaneously moving the ribs outward so
that the chest expands like a barrel. You can check yourself by placing
one hand on the inverted "V" area between the ribs and the other
hand on one side of the lower ribs. Both hands should move outward.
Be sure to keep your shoulders relaxed.

✳ EXERCISE 6: INHALATIONS

PURPOSE: To gain control over rib and diaphragm muscles.

a. Breathe in through your nose as if you are smelling the delightful fra-
   grance of a rose or your favorite cookies baking in the oven. Hold
   the breath and maintain the open-rib-cage position for five slow
   counts. Count silently, not aloud. Exhale through the mouth, collapsing the ribs. Repeat several times.

b. Breathe in through the mouth as if you are sipping a drink through a
   straw. Use short, repeated "sips" until you feel comfortably full of
   air. *Never* take in so much air that you feel "stuffed" or uncom-
   fortably filled. Hold the breath and the expanded chest position for
   five counts. Relax and release the air.

c. Take a deep breath through the mouth as if you are sobbing. Feel the
   air quickly fill up the chest, making certain that the expansion occurs
   low at the waist. Exhale by relaxing the ribs and diaphragm.

d. Inhale by quickly moving the ribs outward (opening the rib cage)
   and simultaneously lowering the diaphragm (relaxing the abdominal
   muscles). Allow the air to enter through the mouth, filling the vacuum created in the lungs. This intake of air is similar to a "sob,"
   but this time don't make any noise, as you probably did in "b"
   and "c" of the exercise. (Remember never to take in so much
   air that it makes you feel uncomfortable.) Exhale by simply relaxing the ribs and diaphragm.

EXERCISE 7: EXHALATIONS

PURPOSE: To discover and gain control over the muscles used in exhalation.
         To learn top control breath for volume.

NOTE: Begin each part of this exercise with a deep inhalation incorporating an expansion of the rib cage with a simultaneous lowering of the diaphragm, thus allowing the air to enter through the mouth and fill the vacuum created in the lungs. Inhale comfortably and deeply and avoid taking in more air than feels comfortable. Perform all the exhalation exercises lying on the floor until you are confident that they are being performed correctly. Then practice the exercises while standing with good posture.

    a. Imagine that there is a candle situated about one foot in front of your lips. Inhale. Hold your breath for three counts (Count at the rate of TWO COUNTS PER SECOND. This approximates a metronome mark of 120 times per second, a march tempo.), then exhale quickly through your mouth, relaxing the ribs all at once. As you exhale, pretend that you are blowing out the candle with a quick rush of air.

    b. Imagine that you are sitting at a table containing a large birthday cake with fifty candles. Inhale. Hold the inhalation for three counts and then blow out all the imaginary candles with a slower, controlled, continuous, thin stream of air (instead of a quick rush of air as in the previous exercise). Blow out the candles without immediately collapsing the rib cage. Allow the rib cage to lower *gradually* and stay aware consciously of the muscular activity of the abdominal muscles of exhalation.

✳   c. Inhale deeply. Blow out the air very slowly and steadily, keeping the ribs *completely open* and *motionless* for as long as you can. Then while continuing the exhalation, gradually allow the rib cage to relax until, at last, you achieve a state of rest. Do not exhale beyond this point.

NOTE: Many people are suprised at how long they can sustain an open rib cage and at how little movement is exerted in the abdominal muscles. This occurs because of the *balanced interaction* of the muscles used in inhalation and exhalation during the expulsion of a gentle, steady stream of air. It is the *correct breathing method for singing*.

✳   d. Inhale deeply, but this time exhale in sharp, staccato spurts while *keeping the rib cage open* (using the abdomen to control the exhalations). Do not inhale or exhale during the pauses between each spurt, and keep your lips open throughout. Utilizing a blow-pause-blow-pause, etc., pattern, practice the exercise until you can exhale twenty spurts per inhalation without collapsing the ribs. Suspend the breath between spurts by keeping the ribs open. Perform the exercise once; then inhale and repeat the sequence, trying to exhale twenty spurts each time while keeping the rib cage open.

You will notice that a faster, more powerful exhalation involves more abdominal activity. In producing the small exhalation (spurts of breath), the inhalation muscles work in an *antagonistic balance* with the muscles of exhalation and are felt in the small, sharp movements of the abdomen.

✳   e. Inhale deeply. Exhale, making a hissy "s-s-s" sound (like the sound of air escaping from a balloon). Make the sound smooth, steady, and of medium volume. Keep the rib cage open as long as you can, then relax it gradually. Time the length of your exhalation with a clock. An exhalation lasting twenty-five to forty-five seconds is excellent.

NOTE: Up to now, we have practiced the proper method for breathing in singing, but we have not used any phonation (vocal sounds). Since the [s] sound does not involve a vibration of the vocal cords, it is not a phonated sound. The purpose of beginning breath exercises with unvoiced sounds was to become acquainted with and gain control of the musculature involved in inhalation and exhalation. Once that is accomplished, the student of singing is ready to co-ordinate the use of the breath with the sound-producing mechanism.

To produce an attractive, free vocal tone requires a special co-ordination of breath with adjustments of the vibrator and the resonators. The following exercises, which involve the use of the [z] sound, provide a start in that direction. In the production of the [z] sound, the vocal cords vibrate and phonation (pitch) is produced.

     f. Inhale deeply. Then exhale, sustaining the consonant [z], as in the word "zeal," at a soft level of volume. Sustain the [z] as long as possible and time the duration of this phonated exhalation. It should approximate the length of time you sustained the unvoiced [s] sound. Keep your rib cage open as long as is comfortable.

   g. PURPOSE: To learn to use breath economically.
                  To learn not to waste air during pauses.
                  To learn to resist the rapid expulsion of breath.
                  To suspend the breath.

Inhale moderately. Count aloud the numbers indicated below. Speak in a moderate tempo (a march-like tempo), using a medium volume. Count easily, without any pressure and tension in the neck. *Do not inhale or exhale during the pauses.* Each pause should last the same length of time as a single count. Count, pause, count, pause, etc., allowing a slow, gradual relaxation of the ribs. Begin the sequence by inhaling only as much air as is needed to complete the exercise. ("P" stands for "pause.")

1 2 3 (P) 4 5 6 7 (P) 8 9 10 (P) 11 12 13 14 15 INHALE
1 2 3 4 (P) 5 6 (P) 7 8 9 10 (P) 11 12 13 (P) 14 15 INHALE

Perform the following sequences. Begin with a moderate inhalation and maintain a good, firm, medium volume level THROUGHOUT each sequence. (A slash "/" indicates a "pause" and an "(I)" indicates "inhalation")

1 2 3 4 5 / 6 7 / 8 9 10 / 11 12 13 / 14 15 (I)
1 2 3 / 4 5 6 7 / 8 9 10 11 / 12 13 / 14 15 (I)

✳   h. Inhale comfortably. Sing the melody of "Swing Low, Sweet Chariot," using a sustained [z] instead of the words. Sing a *continuous* [z], sound (z-z-z-z), *not* a series of repeated "zee" sounds, to substitute for each word. Sing the melody with a quality that is calm, soft, steady, gentle, smooth, lyrical. Replenish your breath only when indicated by the (I) symbol for inhalation. Keep the rib cage open as long as it is comfortable, then allow it to relax *gradually*. Maintain the same volume throughout each phrase in order that your voice does not fade out toward the end. You should never feel as if you have "run out" of breath. Remember: Use a sustained [z] instead of singing the words.

Example:

Swing low, sweet chariot
[z] - - - - - - - - - - - - - - - - - (I)

Coming for to carry me home,
[z] - (I)

Swing low, sweet chariot
[z] - - - - - - - - - - - - - - - - (I)

Coming for to carry me home.
[z] - (I)

Repeat the exercise again, this time using a HUM (instead of the [z]). Hum on the speech sound [m], as in the word "me."

Example:

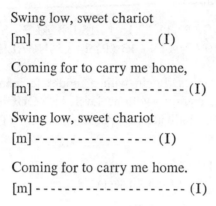

Swing low, sweet chariot
[m] - - - - - - - - - - - - - - - - - (I)

Coming for to carry me home,
[m] - (I)

Swing low, sweet chariot
[m] - - - - - - - - - - - - - - - (I)

Coming for to carry me home.
[m] - (I)

✳   i. Use a similar procedure in the following song. First, sing the melody of the entire song on [z]; second, humming the [m]; and, third, singing the lyrics. Notice that the phrases (the melody line between the inhalations) are longer in this song than in the above song. But still keep the melody continuous and flowing between inhalations. Use a medium-soft volume level and breathe only where indicated by (I). Inhale deeply and comfortably. Keep the rib cage open as long as it's comfortable, then relax slowly. This will create a long, lovely musical phrase, one that is easy to maintain when the breathing is performed properly.

Example: The First Noel

Sing the melody: 1.   z _____ , (I) z _____ , (I)

Hum the melody: 2.   m _____ , (I) m _____ , (I)

Sing the words: 3.   The first Noel, (I) the angels did say, (I)

1. z _____ . (I)

2. m _____ . (I)

3. Was to certain poor shepherds in fields where they lay. (I)

1. z _____ (I)

2. m _____ (I)

3. In fields where they lay keeping their sheep (I)

1. z _____ . (I)

2. m _____ . (I)

3. On a cold winter's night that was so deep. (I)

1. z _____ , (I) z _____ . (I)

2. m _____ , (I) m _____ . (I)

3. Noel, Noel, (I) Noel, Noel. (I)

1. z _____ . (I)

2. m _____ . (I)

3. Born is the King of Israel. (I)

✳   j. Inhale comfortably. Sing this exercise twice—once on [z] and on [m].
First, sing seven [z's] on a single pitch, with a pause between each [z].
Do not allow the rib cage to collapse and do not inhale or exhale
during the pauses. This is a short pattern and you should have considerable breath remaining in the lungs when you have completed the
seventh [z]. Without relaxing the rib cage (don't let it collapse!), replenish the air you have used. Repeat several times. You will notice
that this breath movement occurs mainly with the abdominal muscles

since the rib cage remains almost stationary after the initial inhalation.

Example:

1. z,   z,   z,   z,   z,   z,   z.
2. m,   m,   m,   m,   m,   m,   m.

NOTE: Pauses within a phrase and inhalations at the end of phrases are frequently indicated in written music by the 𝄾 musical notation used above. Appropriately, it is called a REST.

IV. Laryngeal Freedom

The exercise in this section is intended to help you become aware of physical sensations in the larynx.

EXERCISE 8: OPPOSITES

PURPOSE: To experience the difference between hypertension and hypotension in the larynx.

a. Breathe in. Hold your breath and pretend you are lifting a heavy weight. Notice the tightness in the throat. Then grunt, allowing your breath to escape all at once.

In this portion of the exercise, you experienced extreme laryngeal hypertension. The throat was closed off totally and the larynx squeezed shut.

b. Inhale deeply, and then hold your breath for a moment by squeezing the larynx closed. Release the larynx just enough to allow you to speak the following sentence. The quality of your voice will be very strained.

"My throat is very constricted and tight!"

This, too, is another example of laryngeal *hyper*tension (constriction).

c. Inhale gently and sigh *breathily,* feeling a physical and emotional release during the sigh. Loosen your jaw, neck, and shoulders.

This is an example of *hypo*tension (an insufficient amount of tension to accomplish a given task).

d. Inhale gently and sigh, *without being breathy*. Make a clear, gentle, child-like sound.

This "voiced" sigh is produced by a good laryngeal balance that is necessary in the production of an attractive *piano* (soft) singing tone.

e. Say the following sentence aloud, in a tone of voice that is angry and firm:

"Amy, EAT your apple; don't PLAY with it!"

Did you pronounce the first two words percussively, using a sharp, explosive sound for emphasis? This type of harsh emphasis in the initiation of a sound originates in the larynx and is called a GLOTTAL PLOSIVE ATTACK. It involves a hypertense use of the vocal cords and is frequently used in speech for emphasis or to separate a pair of vowels (e.g., "re-*e*nergize," "the *e*nemy").

f. Say the following sentences aloud, in a medium-to-loud volume (as if you are speaking to someone across a large room).

1. "Archie always anticipates energetic exercises."
2. "Oranges and apples are excellent edibles."
3. "Everybody antagonizes Aunt Alice's ostrich."
4. "Andy always arrives after Eddie."

How many glottal plosives did you use in each sentence? More than two is too many because when we employ an excessive number of glottal plosive attacks in speech, we run the risk of tiring the vocal cords and using the larynx unhealthily.

g. Repeat the sentences in a medium-loud volume, trying not to use more
    than two glottal plosives in each sentence.

h. Repeat the sentences, trying to avoid the use of any glottal plosives.
    Speak gently, without emphasizing any of the words.

NOTE: In singing, we should never use a glottal plosive attack except in the
rare instances when we want to sing a percussive, unsustained sound to make
a special effect. Glottal plosives are very hard on the vocal cords, and this
type of hypertensive attack destroys the subsequent production of a free, sustained singing tone. In forthcoming exercises, designed to discover a good
attack of sound in singing (called "on the breath" attack), you will learn
how to achieve emphasis in other, nonharmful ways.

V. Attack

ATTACK is a term that refers to the initiation of a singing tone. Vocal
skills are most evident at the moment of attack when the balance between
all muscles of the sound-producing mechanism needs to be well-managed.
Consequently, every accomplished singer spends a great deal of time practicing, perfecting, and habituating good vocal attacks.

✳ EXERCISE 9: THE "AH" VOWEL SOUND (WHISPERED)

PURPOSE: To produce the correct "ah" vowel sound.

VOWEL: The sound of "ah" (as most people in the United States say in
   the words "father, box, legato, staccato, stop, papa").

PITCH: None. (A whisper has no pitch.)

VOLUME: A gentle, soft whisper.

NOTE: We begin with a whispered "ah" in order to establish the easiest way
to enunciate the vowel. Maintain a good posture while keeping your shoulders, neck, and articulators relaxed. When you whisper "ah," there should
be no hypertension in the muscles of the neck, jaw, lips, or tongue. The jaw
should be in a dropped position and the mouth opened in an oval shape.
The tip of the tongue should touch the back of the bottom front teeth and
should be soft in texture, with no dips. As you begin the whispered sound,
make *no movement* of the tongue. Most importantly . . . do NOT begin the
whispered vowel with a glottal plosive attack. If you have difficulty elimi-

nating the glottal plosive, try whispering "ha" (as in the word *"hot"*) instead of "ah."

PROCEDURE: Stand, or sit, with good posture. Inhale comfortably and deeply. Whisper seven short "ah" vowels, suspending the breath during the pauses between the whispered vowels and keeping the rib cage open throughout. Do not inhale or exhale during the pauses. (A slash "/" indicates a "pause.")

Example:

ah / ah / ah / ah / ah / ah / ah

Inhale, and repeat the exercise again.
Repeat a total of three times.

EXERCISE 10: BREATHY "AH" PRODUCTION

PURPOSE: To avoid vocal strain by using a breathy vocal production on the vowel "ah."

VOWEL: The sound of "ah," as most people say in the words, "*father, box, pop.*"

PITCH: Any comfortable pitch.

VOLUME: Soft.

PROCEDURE: Transfer the method of enunciation used in the whispered "ah" vowel to a breathy production. Sing seven short breathy "ah" vowels, suspending the breath during the pauses. This breathy sound is produced gently, easily, without strain, and definitely should not sound hoarse. It is the sound many people use when they sigh.

Example:

Repeat three times.

❋ EXERCISE 11: "ON THE BREATH" ATTACK

PURPOSE: To establish a good attack.

VOWEL: "Ah."

PITCH: Any comfortable pitch (one that is near to where you speak).
Start the sound directly on the chosen pitch. Don't "slide" into it.

TIMBRE: A conversational speech-type sound, with a clear tonal quality
that is firmly voiced but neither harsh nor breathy.

DURATION: The sounds are short and separated by brief pauses.

DESCRIPTION: Keep your mouth open between each short, detached,
spoken "ah." Keep the rib cage in an open position throughout and use
the "on the breath" attack. A good attack feels firm but not harsh, and
there is no evidence of hypertension.

PROCEDURE: Stand with good posture. Inhale comfortably and deeply.
(Singers usually breathe through the mouth because it is faster.) Sing
seven short "ah's," each one on the same pitch. Remember not to inhale
or exhale between "ah's."

Example:

Sing fully voiced.

ah,   ah,   ah,   ah,   ah,   ah,   ah.

Relax . . . inhale again and repeat the exercise three or more times.
When you repeat the exercise, try to make each "ah" even *shorter* but
do not speed up the tempo.

NOTE: A musical note of very short duration, when separated by a pause
from the next note, is called a STACCATO note. In written music, it is no-
tated by a dot placed above the note.

If you have access to a piano, or other pitch-producing instrument, try
singing the pattern a half step higher or lower.

Example:

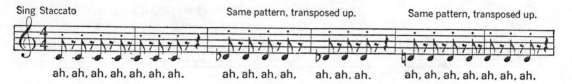

Sing Staccato   Same pattern, transposed up.   Same pattern, transposed up.

ah, ah, ah, ah, ah, ah, ah.   ah, ah, ah, ah,   ah, ah, ah.   ah, ah, ah, ah, ah, ah, ah.

✱ EXERCISE 12: STACCATO NOTES (5–3–1 PATTERN)

PURPOSE: To build toward a good attack.

Sing on "ah" the following musical pattern of notes (called a 5 – 3 – 1 pattern) in a staccato fashion. Start on any pitch that is comfortable for you. The pattern sounds like the first three notes of the song "Dixie": "*O, I wish* I was in the land of cotton . . ."

Example:

Pattern: 5 – 3 – 1

O   I   wish I   was ___ in the   land   of   cot - ton

NOTE: The 5 – 3 – 1 numbers in the title of this musical pattern correspond to the numbers of the notes in a major scale—"5" being the fifth note of the scale (sol), "3" being the third (mi), and "1" being the tonic note (do).

Repeat the pattern several times, using the same pitches or transposing to pitches slightly higher or lower than the original pattern. If you can accompany yourself on a piano, start each repeated pattern a half step higher than the one before, until you are singing as high as you can sing comfortably. Then reverse and sing each pattern a half step lower than the one before.

Example:

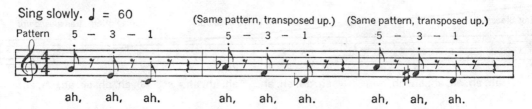

To perform the staccato 5 – 3 – 1 exercise successfully (maintaining good attack and accurate pitch control) will necessitate adequate breath control from the abdominal muscles and careful vowel enunciation.

NOTE: The following series of attack exercises include several basic musical patterns which can be used in a variety of different vocal exercises. Learning these basic patterns, and their names, expedites the study of voice.

Unless otherwise indicated, all forthcoming exercises in this chapter should be repeated on different pitches, up and down the vocal scale (incorporating a high-low range that is comfortable for you) in order to exercise your voice fully. You will find it easier if you use a piano or other pitch device to assist you in finding the relative pitches. A pitch pipe, for example, can be used to establish the beginning pitch on each musical pattern and may be purchased for approximately six dollars at any well-stocked music store. However, it is not mandatory to use specific pitches. If you don't have a musical instrument available, just sing some patterns higher and some lower.

The object of these exercises is to practice a particular vocal response on a variety of different pitches . . . ultimately on pitches that span the entire range of your voice. Begin with pitches that you find easy and comfortable. After you experience "on the breath" singing and a reduction of hypotension and hypertension, the extreme high and low pitches will become as easy as the middle-range pitches with which you are now most comfortable.

✳ EXERCISE 13: STACCATO NOTES (FULL OCTAVE OF A MAJOR SCALE)

PURPOSE: To build toward a good attack.

Using the "ah" vowel in a staccato manner, sing the following 8 – 7 – 6 – 5 – 4 – 3 – 2 – 1 musical pattern, which is a full octave major scale (descending).

The pattern of notes is the same as those at the beginning of the hymn "Joy to the World." However, sing the pattern with notes of equal duration (note value) instead of to the rhythm of "Joy to the World." Use "on the breath" attack and maintain the same vowel position and enunciation as you descend the scale.

Example:

Repeat the pattern, starting on both higher and lower pitches.

✳ EXERCISE 14: LEGATO NOTES (5-4-3-2-1 PATTERN)

PURPOSE: To build toward a good attack.

Sing, on "ah," the last five notes of the above full-scale pattern, and sustain the final note for as long as you can maintain the open-rib-cage position.

Sit or stand with good posture; breathe comfortably and deeply; use "on the breath" attack; and maintain a good "ah" position and a free, open throat as you descend the scale. Sing very *legato*, using no pauses between notes and singing a smooth, continuous melody line. Sing with a medium volume.

Example:

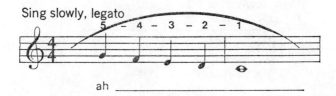

Repeat, starting on higher and lower pitches.

❋ EXERCISE 15: STACCATO NOTES (3–2–1 PATTERN)

PURPOSE: To build good vocal attack.

Sing "ah," staccato fashion, on a 3 – 2 – 1 pattern (the first three notes of the song "Three Blind Mice"). Use good posture and maintain an open throat. Sing "on the breath."

Example:

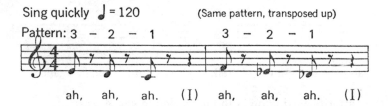

Repeat, transposing to other pitches.

❋ EXERCISE 16: DETACHED 3–2–1 PATTERN

Use "ah" and the 3–2–1 pattern, but this time slow the tempo and hold each note longer than you did in the above exercise. Make each note and each pause between notes last an equal length of time.

Don't exhale or inhale between notes (suspend the breath!). Although the notes are detached from one another, they are no longer considered staccato (of very short duration) because they are being sustained longer. The (I) indicates "inhalation."

Example:

Repeat on other pitches.

✻ EXERCISE 17: LEGATO 3−2−1 PATTERN

Sing the 3−2−1 pattern on "ah," in a *legato* fashion. **Legato** is the process of singing smoothly from one note to another without interruption. Use a smooth, steady, sustained musical line, without any pauses between notes, and hold the final note as long as you can without losing breath position.

Example:

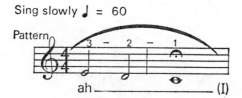

Repeat on other pitches.

NOTE: The preceding exercises are valuable in learning how to make the transition from singing staccato notes to singing more sustained tones, and finally to singing long, smooth (legato) melodies. It is important to remember that we attack a note every time we initiate a sound after an inhalation or a suspended breath. Regardless of whether the note is short or long in duration, we must still pay close attention to how we start the sound. Therefore, always sing "on the breath" while practicing these exercises.

In singing note patterns on "ah," the greatest efficiency in production is achieved by keeping the mouth open between notes. However, we must also remember that all of the sound-producing mechanism (including the mouth) must remain flexible, unrigid and ready to move at all times. The same holds true for the rib cage, which also must remain open (without being rigid) and always in dynamic muscular balance. If you feel any rigidity in the chest, allow your rib cage to relax slightly. A feeling of rigidity indicates that the muscle adjustment has become static.

EXERCISE 18: STACCATO VERSUS LEGATO

PURPOSE: To contrast staccato and legato performances.

a. Staccato

Using a comfortable pitch and a slow tempo, sing the entire melody of "Three Blind Mice" in a *staccato* fashion, using "ah" in place of the words. Maintain "on the breath" attack throughout the song and inhale only where indicated by (I). Be sure to inhale correctly and to keep the ribs open during exhalation. You should feel sharp abdominal muscle movement when singing the staccato notes. Maintain an open throat and a well-enunciated "ah." Keep the mouth open throughout the song.

Example:

THREE BLIND MICE

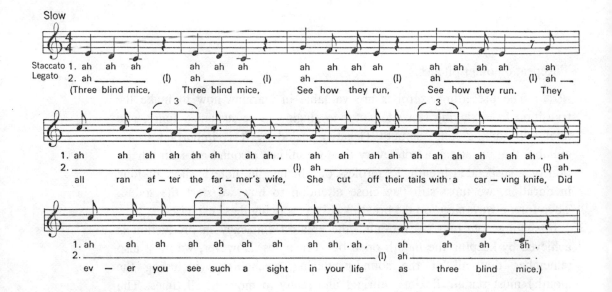

b. Legato

Singing again on "ah," repeat the above procedure, but this time sing the notes in a legato fashion (without pausing between notes). Keep an even intensity of tone (a medium-loud volume) throughout each phrase. Do not allow the last note of the phrase to fade in volume. Make the melody even, smooth, and steady. Inhale only where indicated by (I).

VI. Voicing

VOICING is a term used in singing to refer to the degree to which the vocal cords come together during the production of sound. The various degrees of adjustment range from the open-cord situation of a whisper (in which no pitch is produced), to the partial closure in producing breathy sounds and, finally, to being firmly closed in fully voiced, efficient sound production.

EXERCISE 19: FROM WHISPERED TO BREATHY TO FULLY VOICED

PURPOSE: To experience the degrees of voicing.
            To accomplish a fully voiced tone.

a. Whisper seven "ah's" to establish good vowel enunciation. (A slash "/" indicates a "pause.")

Example:

ah / ah / ah / ah / ah / ah / ah

b. Maintaining the kinesthetic memory of the whispered "ah," sing three breathy 1 – 2 – 3 – 2 – 1 patterns. Sing the three patterns continuously, without pausing to inhale. Be sure the "ah" is well-enunciated and that there is no hypertension in the lips, jaw, and tongue.

Example:

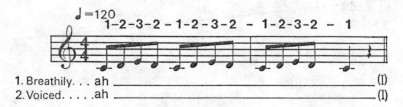

♩=120
1-2-3-2 - 1-2-3-2 - 1-2-3-2 - 1

1. Breathily. . . ah _____ (I)
2. Voiced. . . . . ah _____ (I)

    c. Sing the same pattern using a fully voiced "ah" and an "on the breath" attack.

VII. Registration

Occasionally "breaks" occur in the voice because the singer does not maintain a proper, balanced adjustment of the vocal cords as he sings up or down a scale. The following exercises are designed to help singers even out their voice (called "blending the registers"), increase range, improve the ease of singing, and eliminate weak spots.

NOTE: The term REGISTRATION refers to specific modes of adjustment of all the laryngeal muscles involved in the production of any particular pitch and volume. Singers are primarily concerned with two types of registers— **LIGHT** and **HEAVY.** The light register adjustment produces a very distinct tonal quality which is light, flute-like, pure of sound and weak in intensity (except at the top of the vocal range, where it becomes louder in volume). In men, light registration is known as "falsetto," and in women, it is their upper pitch range. The heavy register adjustment is characterized by a distinct tonal quality that is heavy, firm, deep, and resembles the quality of normal adult speech. "Breaks" occur in the singing voice when either the light or heavy register adjustment is used inappropriately and incorrectly.

Light and heavy registrations can be produced with or without hypertension. If they are produced with hypertension and rigidity, the resulting adjustment is STATIC and undesirable in singing. When produced without hypertension, the adjustment is FREE and beneficial in learning to sing. By discovering and exercising free light and heavy registrations, the singer learns to relate desired tone quality to specific physical adjustments. He also learns to control specific adjustments of the intrinsic laryngeal muscles.

✳ EXERCISE 20: LIGHT REGISTRATION

PURPOSE: To discover free light registration.

Sigh as lightly and softly as you can, on "ah," using an "on the breath" attack. Begin on a very high pitch (men, use your falsetto) and maintain a free relaxed throat and full voicing. Your goal is to produce a gentle sigh without any hypertension and to experience an emotional and physical release. If you find that the tip of the tongue wants to pull backward or that the back of the tongue wants to drop downward, don't let it! Instead, keep the tongue forward, with the tip touching the back of the bottom front teeth.

The sigh should be fully voiced, gentle, and soft. It should sound clear, bell-like, and perhaps even child-like.

Example:

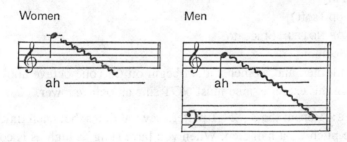

NOTE: In this exercise the tongue must not be allowed to drop down in back nor to be flat nor to have any dips or grooves. You may have heard singers use the term "grooved tongue," which describes a physical response sometimes used in more advanced exercises. It is the wrong response for this exercise.

It should be apparent now that vocal exercises always build upon earlier exercises. Therefore, when performing a new exercise, it is necessary to maintain and incorporate the correct responses learned in previous exercises.

✳ EXERCISE 21: LIGHT REGISTRATION

PURPOSE: To practice free light registration.

NOTE: Both men and women can produce light registration freely and without hypertension from the highest pitches they can sing down to G_3 (see piano keyboard on the following page. Men are often able to take light registration down as low as C_3! In light registration, the lower the sung pitch, the softer the sound becomes. Around middle C the sound is very soft, and on pitches lower than middle C the sounds become so soft they are barely audible. To sing these lower pitches more loudly requires a different adjustment that is no longer in light registration.

If the singer is to become accomplished in the usage of dynamic blends, he will find this exercise extremely useful. Practicing a free light register adjustment on all pitches, especially on the lower notes, eventually develops a smooth vocal line and a good high range.

PATTERN: 3−2−1 ("Three Blind Mice")
VOWEL: "Ah"
VOLUME: pp (soft)
DURATION OF NOTES: Staccato
TEMPO: Medium
PITCH: Both men and women should begin on C_5 (one octave above middle C). In this exercise, men must NOT sing an octave lower.

PROCEDURE: Repeat the 3−2−1 pattern several times, but each time transpose the pitch up a half step. When you have sung as high as is comfortable, then reverse and sing the pattern a half step down each time until you have sung as low as is comfortable. *Maintain light registration.*

Example:

NOTE: Since this exercise is best accomplished with the use of specific pitches, you will need assistance from a pitch-producing instrument. Any in-

strument will do, including a piano, guitar, pitch pipe, etc. The following il-
lustration of a piano keyboard is marked with an "x" to indicate the $3-2-1$
pattern.

(If you do not have an instrument available, change the procedure.
Starting on any high pitch, using "ah," sigh with the gentle, child-like
quality of light registration. Let the pitch of your voice slur downward
to the lowest note you can produce with that *same quality*.)

Example:

PIANO KEYBOARD

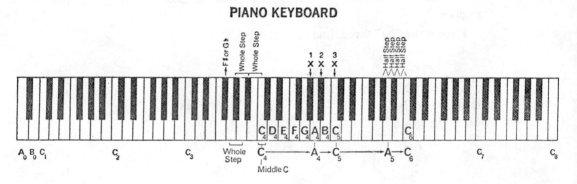

On the piano, a half step is the distance between each adjoining note
(whether black or white). A whole step is composed of two half steps. "Three
Blind Mice" (the $3-2-1$ pattern) is composed of three notes joined together
consecutively by two descending whole steps. Therefore, the same pattern
emerges no matter what note we start on, as long as we continue by playing
two whole steps downward (to the left on the piano keyboard).

To **transpose** a pattern a half step upward, we play each pitch a half step
higher (to the right on the keyboard). Conversely, transposing a half step
downward means to play each note a half step lower on the piano.

Each black note has two names, with the names derived from the particular
note that it adjoins. The black note immediately adjoining the *F* note, on the
right, is *F♯* (*F* sharp). If we consider the same note as being to the left of
the *G* note, it is called *G♭* (*G* flat). **"Flat"** indicates an adjoining black note
on the left (lower), and **"sharp"** indicates an adjoining black note on the right
(higher).

✲ EXERCISE 22: HEAVY REGISTRATION

PURPOSE: To discover free heavy registration.

Speak loudly on "ha," on the pitch A_3, using a firm, clear tone. The tone must not be strained, muffled, breathy, or throaty. (Some singers refer to this sound as "chest voice" or "normal voice.")

Speak "from the abdomen" using an "on the breath attack" . . . *not* glottal plosive! Be sure that you say "ha," not "huh" or "haw" or some other variation. In this exercise, also be sure to keep your jaw dropped lower than it normally is in speech. Women should speak on low pitches.

Repeat the "ha" three times vigorously.

Example:

ha / ha / ha
ha / ha / ha
ha / ha / ha

✲ EXERCISE 23: HEAVY REGISTRATION

PURPOSE: To practice free heavy registration.

NOTE: This exercise is of great value to singers because it builds power in singing.

PATTERN: 3 – 2 – 1

VOWEL: "Ah"

VOLUME: f (loud)

DURATION OF NOTES: Staccato

TEMPO: Medium

PITCH: *This is the only exercise in which you must observe a limitation in pitch. Do not sing any higher than E_4!* This exact pitch applies to both men and women. For men, the E_4 pitch occurs in their high range; for women, in their low range. Sing only as high as E_4, then reverse and sing the pattern as low as is comfortable.

PROCEDURE: Begin the pattern on a pitch in your low speaking range and maintain heavy registration throughout the exercise. Transpose in the manner indicated below to pitches up to E_4 (not any higher!), then down as low as you can sing comfortably.

Example:

EXERCISE 24: BLENDING THE REGISTERS

PURPOSE: To blend the two extreme registers.

NOTE: Although the extreme adjustments of the light and heavy registers are rarely used in singing (except for special effects), singers practice these two extreme adjustments in order to develop their widest range and to develop the flexibility to BLEND the extreme qualities. A blended voice, from top to bottom pitch, is the ultimate technical goal of serious voice students. In learning to blend light and heavy registers, singers also learn to create other specific laryngeal adjustments and tonal qualities which eventually result in the production of a smooth vocal line and maximum control, ease, and power.

PATTERN: Sigh, allowing the voice to slide downward in pitch.

VOWEL: "Ah"

VOLUME: Begin softly; end more loudly.

DURATION: Sigh slowly, sliding downward without hurry.

PITCH: Start as high as is comfortable. End on a note near the bottom of your vocal range.

PROCEDURE:

Step 1 — Begin the sigh in light registration. Allow your voice to descend in pitch to your low range, letting the low notes become louder. Heavy registration will emerge with the increase in volume on the low notes. Allow the change in registration to be abrupt in this step. Let the "break" occur.

Step 2 — Sigh, slurring downward, and this time *sigh very softly as you pass through the Middle C area.* Do not allow the break to occur; instead, change into heavy registration imperceptibly as you reach the lower notes. It is possible to do this by sighing *very softly.*

Step 3 — Sigh, slurring downward, sighing *louder* this time in the range from A_4 to A_3, ending with a firm tone (in heavy register) on the bottom notes. Ideally, there should be no audible "break," or any physical sensation of transition.

NOTE: Repeat this exercise many, many times. Steps one and two should be practiced faithfully over a period of weeks before proceeding to step three. Eventually, you should maintain a consistent volume throughout the sigh (from top to bottom) without any weak spots or breaks.

The exercise presents somewhat more of a challenge to men than to women, because for men (especially baritones and basses) the physical change from light to heavy registration is more pronounced. Men should practice steps one and two of the exercise by carrying light registration down to *very* low pitches (F_3 or below).

Gradually, as you incorporate step three, you will discover that you can *begin* the sigh louder. After a period of time, men will discover they no longer need to use a pure falsetto at the top of their range; instead, they will establish a quality that has more weight and a fuller color, especially as they begin to use the "yawn-sigh" method used in upcoming exercises.

There are numerous other exercises designed to establish good, functional blends. But those exercises—built upon arpeggios and scale work—are more advanced and require a considerable amount of pianistic skill. Because they also require instruction and observation from a voice teacher, they are not being included here.

VIII. Vertical Larynx Position

One of the major differences between skilled and unskilled singers is the position of the larynx in the throat as they sing up and down the scale. A beginning singer tends to raise the larynx on high notes until, eventually, he feels a squeeze in his throat and sounds as if he is choking. A skilled singer has learned to keep the larynx comfortably low in the throat while singing higher notes. This laryngeal adjustment (called the VERTICAL LARYNX POSITION) results in the production of high notes that are attractive to the listener and are produced easily with little, or no, sensation in the singer's throat.

EXERCISE 25: VERTICAL LARYNX POSITION

PURPOSE: To discover vertical larynx position.

1. To feel your larynx, place your hand on your throat, just under the jaw. (A man can locate his larynx easily by placing his hand on his Adam's apple.) Now, swallow and feel the up-and-down movement in the throat. What you actually feel is the up-and-down motion of the larynx.
2. Now yawn (with your hand on the throat) and feel the downward movement of the larynx.
3. Yawn again; then sigh, leaving the larynx down. Your throat will feel open and, perhaps, somewhat stretched.
4. Begin to yawn . . . but just *begin* it. (Don't allow the larynx to lower as drastically as in a full yawn; don't feel the extreme stretch of a complete yawn.) Inhale as if you are beginning to yawn, thus lowering the larynx, then sigh while maintaining the open throat feeling. Repeat several times. Keep the tip of the tongue forward.

NOTE: The exercise will help you discover the comfortable, rather low larynx position called an OPEN THROAT. Open throat is easily maintained on lower pitches and must be maintained on higher ones as well. The open-throat sensation stems more from the low position of the larynx than from the wide diameter of the throat. It is important not to "force" the larynx downward as this would result in an undesirable, hypertensive, depressed larynx position.

❋ EXERCISE 26: YAWN-SIGH

PURPOSE: To practice an open throat by maintaining a comfortably low larynx position.

VOWEL: "Ah"
VOLUME: Medium-soft
PITCH: Start on a high pitch
TEMPO: Slow
PATTERN: Descending slurred sigh

PROCEDURE:

Step 1 — Inhale, starting a yawn.

Step 2 — Sigh, while making certain that the larynx remains low, but not depressed downward. (If you notice a slight change in the pure "ah" enunciation, don't be concerned. This happens in the yawn-sigh exercise. The high notes will have a fuller quality.) Keep the tip of the tongue forward.

Step 3 — Repeat several times, each time starting on the same pitch or on an even higher pitch if you can do so comfortably.

✸ EXERCISE 27:   OPEN THROAT / LOW LARYNX

PURPOSE: To maintain an open throat while singing a complete melody, thereby avoiding a feeling of strain on higher pitches and gaining power and warmth in the voice.

VOWEL: Use "ah" in place of the words of the song.

PATTERN: Sing the melody of the song "Three Blind Mice," using a good legato line.

PITCH: Start on a comfortable pitch.

TEMPO: Slow

VOLUME: Loud

PROCEDURE: Use a good breathing procedure and keep the rib cage open. Repeat the procedure used in the legato singing of "Three Blind Mice" (as found in Exercise 18 on page 148) with the following differences:

1. Sing the melody with a pensive, sad attitude.
2. Use warm, full, dramatic tones.
3. The "ah" should have a yawn-like quality.
4. Keep the larynx low even on higher pitches.
5. Repeat, starting on a higher pitch.

✸ EXERCISE 28:   OPEN THROAT / LOW LARYNX

PURPOSE: To maintain an open-throat position.

Now that you can control your larynx from bobbing up whenever you sing a high note, repeat Exercise 27. This time, however, sing the

"Three Blind Mice" melody using the pure "ah" vowel enunciation instead of the yawn-like "ah." Sing with a happy, cheerful attitude and a bright, clear tonal quality. Continue to keep the larynx low, calm, and relatively still throughout. Again, keep the larynx comfortably low; to *depress* it is even *worse* than letting it bob upward.

NOTE: Do you know what accounts for the difference between the warmer sound of Exercise 27 and the brighter sound of Exercise 28? It is the difference between the way the "ah" vowel was enunciated in each reading of the song.

IX. Vowels

All singing is produced on sounds that originate within a language structure. Occasionally, isolated sounds are used, such as the "clicks" and "hisses" found in some contemporary art music, but most of the time singing sounds are produced on speech sounds within the language structure of vowels and consonants.

Because every word contains a vowel, and because melody is accomplished on sustained vowel sounds, a singer must learn to enunciate vowels correctly in order to achieve control of his vocal tone and the most efficient use of his instrument. He must learn how to shape his resonating cavities in a way that will produce the most efficient vowel sound, one that is produced by the amplification of specific overtones and the filtering out of undesirable inharmonic partials. (Refer to Chapter Four, "Scientific Measurement of Tone Color," for a discussion on the harmonic series, p. 61.)

A vowel is considered well-enunciated when the energy of the tone falls into clearly defined FORMANTS (strong, narrow bands of frequencies) with few inharmonic partials. The mastery of such a vowel production results in singing that is free, easy, healthy, musical, and has the greatest carrying power. For this reason, singers practice the basic production of "pure" vowels every day in their warm-up and technique sessions. In addition to working on "pure" vowels, they learn to change the vowel slightly ("color" the vowel) for the purpose of varying mood, emotion, dialect, tone color, and style.

In the production of vowel sounds, the tongue, jaw, lips, and soft palate are the major parts of the body which shape the resonating cavities. The positioning of these parts, called the ARTICULATORS, must be habituated by singers if they are to attain maximum control, beauty, and expression in their voices. The following exercises are typical of the ones used by every singer to accomplish this goal.

THE VOCAL TRACT

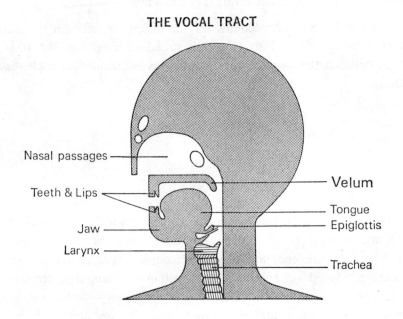

✴ EXERCISE 29: VOWELS

PURPOSE: To discover the positions of the articulators (lips, tongue, and jaw) in the production of the pure "ee," "ah," and "oo" vowels.

a. The "ee" Vowel (as in the word "b*ee*t")

Whisper "ee" gently while looking in a mirror. Your goal is to produce a clear "ee"; therefore, listen carefully to your enunciation. Whisper as gently as possible. Observe the following instructions:

1. Use balanced posture and an "on the breath" attack, *not glottal plosive!* If you have any difficulty achieving an initial gentle flow of air, try using an "h" before the vowel, whispering "he" or "heat."

2. Keep your lips relaxed, especially at the corners of the mouth. Don't pull your lips back into a smile. It isn't necessary to smile when enunciating a pure "ee."

3. Keep your jaw flexible and dropped slightly. Do not clench your jaw.

4. The tip of the tongue should press gently against the back of the bottom front teeth and the middle part of the tongue should be rounded and kept high and forward in the mouth.

5. When you whisper "ee" correctly, you will feel a small stream of air pass lightly over the lower lip. The air passes through a small tunnel between the tongue and the teeth ridge (located just behind the top teeth).

NOTE: The diagram below illustrates the difference in the shape of the mouth during the correct enunciation of each of the vowels being used in this exercise. Notice that in the production of "ee" the tongue divides the front of the mouth from the throat, creating two air cavities joined together by a narrow tunnel. In "ah," however, the mouth and throat become as one cavity, considerably larger in volume and aperture than for "ee." The different shaping of the resonating cavities by the articulators creates a particular formant structure of partials for each vowel. This accounts for the fact that we are able to distinguish one vowel sound from another and for the fact that by properly shaping the resonating cavity we can produce the most efficient enunciation of any vowel.

MOUTH POSITIONS (ee, ah, o͞o)

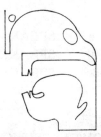

"ee" as in beet   "ah" as in father   "o͞o" as in boot

b. The "ah" Vowel (as in the word "father")

Practice the easiest, clearest enunciation of "ah" by whispering the vowel gently. Listen carefully to the sound you produce and continue to look in a mirror to observe the position of your mouth.

1. Use an "on the breath" attack.
2. Keep your lips relaxed.

3. Drop your jaw (lower than it was for "ee").

4. Keep the tip of the tongue touching the back of the bottom front teeth.

5. Be sure the tongue is soft in texture, with no dips.

c. The "o͞o" Vowel (as in the word "m*oo*n")

Practice whispering the "o͞o" vowel while listening carefully to your sound and looking in a mirror to watch your mouth.

1. Close your jaw more than it was in "ah."

2. Bring the lips forward.

3. Make certain the tip of the tongue touches the back of the bottom front teeth.

❋ EXERCISE 30: VOWELS (WHISPERED AND SPOKEN)

PURPOSE: To transfer the exact enunciation and physical formation of the vowels "ee," "ah," and "o͞o" from a whisper into speech.

PATTERN: Whisper each vowel three times, then speak the same vowel three times.

Example:

WHISPER: ee / ee / ee   SPEAK: ee / ee / ee
WHISPER: ah / ah / ah   SPEAK: ah / ah / ah
WHISPER: o͞o / o͞o / o͞o   SPEAK: o͞o / o͞o / o͞o

❋ EXERCISE 31: VOWELS (SUNG)

PURPOSE: To transfer correct vowel enunciation from a whisper into sing-
            ing.

PATTERN: 1 – 2 – 3 – 2 – 1

PITCH: Begin on a comfortable pitch in your normal speaking range.

TEMPO: Moderate

VOLUME: Medium, on the beginning pitches. Sing more softly as you transpose the pattern higher.

PROCEDURE: (It would be beneficial for you to tape-record your whispered and sung vowels to determine whether they sound the way you want them to.)

1. *Whisper* the vowels three times, while looking in a mirror at the position of the lips, tongue, and jaw.

2. *Sing* each pattern three times, using one breath and one vowel each time. In singing the pattern, use the same mouth position and vowel enunciation as when you whispered.

Example:

Sing: "ee"——————————————————————.
Sing: "ah"——————————————————————.
Sing: "ōō"——————————————————————.

3. Transpose the pattern to other pitches, repeating the entire process.

NOTE: Although our alphabet contains only five letters which are called vowels (a, e, i, o, u), actually there are fifteen basic vowel sounds in the English language. These additional ten sounds are created by various spelling combinations of the original five vowels. In the following list of basic vowel sounds you will encounter phonetic symbols in brackets. The symbols comprise the International Phonetic Alphabet (IPA) in which each particular symbol signifies a particular speech sound. The IPA is applicable in all Western languages.

1. "ee" sound [i] as in "f*ee*"
2. "ih" sound [ɪ] as in "f*i*t"
3. "aye" sound [eɪ] as in "f*a*te"
4. "eh" sound [ɛ] as in "f*e*tter"
5. "ă" sound [æ] as in "f*a*t"
6. "ah" sound [ɑ] as most people say "f*a*ther"
7. "aw" sound [ɔ] as in "f*ou*ght"
8. "oh" sound [oʊ] as in "f*o*e"
9. "ŏŏ" sound [ʊ] as in "f*oo*t"
10. "ōō" sound [u] as in "f*oo*l"
11. "uh" sound [ʌ] or [ə] as in "f*u*ss"
12. "er" sound [ɝ] or [ɚ] as in "f*u*rth*er*"
13. "er" without the "r" quality [ɜ], typical of southern pronunciation in

words such as "*further*, *heard*, *curd*." This vowel sound is frequently used in singing to replace the tenser vowel [ɝ].

14. A bright "ah" [ɑ], used by New Englanders in words like "B*o*ston, f*a*ther, c*a*r."

15. A short "aw" vowel sound [ɒ], used by people who tend to clip words such as "g*o*t, n*o*t, b*o*ther, c*o*t."

✳ EXERCISE 32: VOWEL POSITIONS

PURPOSE: To learn more about vowel positions.

PROCEDURE:

1. Whisper each sample word presented in the above list of basic vowel sounds. Use the ones found in numbers 1 through 12 of the list.

2. Whisper each of the vowel sounds found in numbers 1 through 12, while looking in a mirror to observe the changing positions of the lips, tongue, and jaw.

3. Become aware of the following:

   a. The tip of the tongue remains behind and touching the bottom front teeth on all the vowel sounds *except* number 12.

   b. The lips stay relaxed throughout, but the jaw drops gradually as you progress from number 1 through number 6.

   c. The lips move forward gradually and the jaw closes gradually in numbers 7 through 10.

   d. On the "er" sound in number 12, the tip of the tongue lifts, becoming suspended in the center of the mouth.

✳ EXERCISE 33: FORWARD VOWELS

PURPOSE: To practice forward vowels . . . the vowels found in numbers 1 through 5 of the list of Basic Vowel Sounds. (They are called FORWARD or FRONT vowels because the highest part of the tongue remains forward in the mouth during their proper production.)

PROCEDURE:

1. Whisper each vowel three times; then immediately sing the same vowel seven times on a comfortable single pitch. You should not alter the posi-

MOUTH POSITIONS (ee, ih, aye, eh, a)

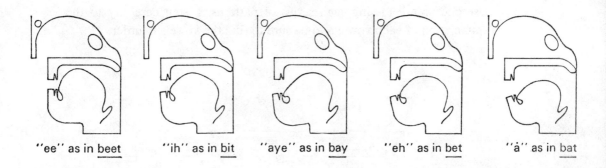

"ee" as in <u>beet</u>   "ih" as in <u>bit</u>   "aye" as in <u>bay</u>   "eh" as in <u>bet</u>   "à" as in <u>bat</u>

tion of the lips, jaw, or tongue when transferring from a whisper to a sung tone. Be sure to use an "on the breath" attack on each repeated vowel sound.

2. Repeat step 1 on each of the forward vowels.

Example:

Slowly

(as in f<u>ee</u>):   1. ee ee ee ee   ee ee ee
(as in f<u>i</u>t):   2. ih ih ih ih   ih ih ih
(as in f<u>a</u>te):   3. aye aye aye aye aye aye aye
(as in f<u>e</u>tter): 4. eh eh eh eh   eh eh eh
(as in f<u>a</u>t):   5. à   à   à   à   à   à   à

Repeat the exercise several more times, using different pitches.

✳ EXERCISE 34: FORWARD VOWELS

PURPOSE: Additional practice on forward vowels.

VOWELS: "ee," "ih," "aye," "eh," "à," "ah"

PATTERN: 1 – 2 – 3 – 2 – 1

STARTING PITCH: Any comfortable pitch.

TEMPO: Quick

VOLUME: Medium

PROCEDURE: Sing the 1−2−3−2−1 pattern three times, legato, on "ee," followed by the same pattern on "ih," "aye," "eh," "à" and "ah." Use one breath to sing each series of patterns. Listen carefully to the enunciation of each vowel and be sure to sing the vowels in order.

Example:

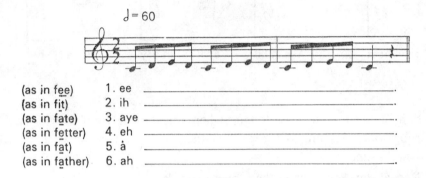

(as in fee)	1. ee	_____.
(as in fit)	2. ih	_____.
(as in fate)	3. aye	_____.
(as in fetter)	4. eh	_____.
(as in fat)	5. à	_____.
(as in father)	6. ah	_____.

Repeat the procedure, transposing a half step upward each time.

✱ EXERCISE 35: BACK VOWELS

PURPOSE: To practice the back vowels. (Back vowels are the vowels found in numbers 6 through 10 of the list of Basic Vowel Sounds. They are called BACK vowels because the highest part of the tongue is in the back section of the mouth. The *tip* of the tongue, however, still remains forward, behind the bottom front teeth.)

MOUTH POSITIONS (aw, oh, o͝o, o͞o)

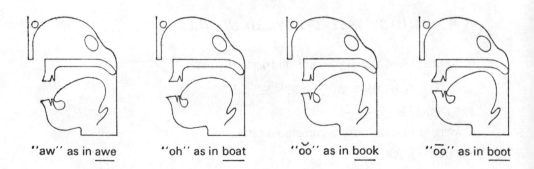

"aw" as in awe   "oh" as in boat   "o͝o" as in book   "o͞o" as in boot

PROCEDURE:

1. Whisper each vowel three times; then immediately sing the same vowel
   seven times on a comfortable single pitch. Listen carefully to the sung
   vowel, making certain that it sounds and looks exactly the same as the
   whispered vowel. Do not change the position of the lips, jaw, or tongue
   when transferring from a whisper to a sung tone.

2. Repeat step 1 on each of the vowels.

Example:

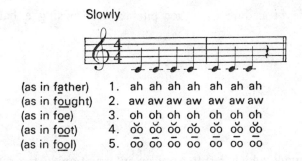

(as in f<u>a</u>ther)	1.	ah	ah	ah	ah	ah	ah	ah
(as in f<u>ou</u>ght)	2.	aw	aw	aw	aw	aw	aw	aw
(as in f<u>oe</u>)	3.	oh	oh	oh	oh	oh	oh	oh
(as in f<u>oo</u>t)	4.	ŏŏ	ŏŏ	ŏŏ	ŏŏ	ŏŏ	ŏŏ	ŏŏ
(as in f<u>oo</u>l)	5.	o͞o	o͞o	o͞o	o͞o	o͞o	o͞o	o͞o

Repeat the exercise several more times using other pitches.

✳ EXERCISE 36: BACK VOWELS

PURPOSE: Additional practice on back vowels.

VOWELS: "ah," "aw," "oh," "ŏŏ," "o͞o"

PATTERN: 1 − 2 − 3 − 2 − 1

STARTING PITCH: Any comfortable pitch.

TEMPO: Quick

VOLUME: Medium

PROCEDURE: Sing the 1 − 2 − 3 − 2 − 1 pattern three times on one breath,
   legato, for each of the vowels. Listen carefully to the enunciation of each
   vowel and be sure to sing the vowels in order.

Example:

(as in f<u>a</u>ther) 1. ah _____.
(as in f<u>ou</u>ght) 2. aw _____.
(as in f<u>oe</u>)   3. oh _____.
(as in f<u>oo</u>t)   4. ŏŏ _____.
(as in f<u>oo</u>l)   5. ōō _____.

Repeat the procedure on other pitches, transposing a half step each time.

X. Consonants

Speech sounds which result from an interruption in the air flow (by the lips, teeth, or tongue) are called **CONSONANTS.** Unlike vowel sounds, which can have considerable volume if they are enunciated properly, consonants have very limited carrying power because of the nature of their production. If spoken and sung words are to be intelligible to a listener, consonants must be articulated with considerable energy and clarity (but with no hypertension!).

There are twenty-five consonant sounds in the English language. Singers need to discover "where" and "how" air flow is interrupted in the production of each consonant sound (called "the place and manner of articulation"), and then they must spend a great deal of time practicing consonant articulation. In this way, singers achieve clarity of sound and the most successful communication of mood, emphasis, style, personality, energy, and emotion in the performance of a song.

✻ EXERCISE 37: CONSONANTS

PURPOSE: To become aware of how consonants are produced and to practice consonant articulation.

Practice the following lists of consonants, consciously noticing "where" and "how" they are produced. Articulate all of the consonants with clarity and energy, but *without* hypertension.

These first two groups of words involve the use of the *lips* in articulating the consonants. Sing on a single, repeated pitch. Then transpose the pitch up or down. (Use the same procedure throughout this exercise.)

Example:

INITIAL CONSONANTS (at the beginning of the word)

"b"	big,	belt,	ba —	by,	boy.	
"p"	Pete,	pat,	pup —	py,	please.	
"f"	fun,	fly,	face,	fool,	phase.	(phase has initial "f" sound)
"v"	vet,	vat,	vine,	vain,	vote.	
"w"	won,	win,	wept,	one,	weep.	(one has initial "w" sound)
"ch"	chin,	child,	cheek,	chick,	chop.	

FINAL CONSONANTS (at the end of the word)

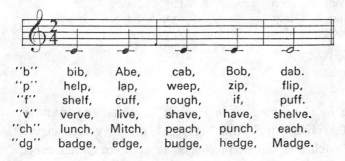

"b"	bib,	Abe,	cab,	Bob,	dab.
"p"	help,	lap,	weep,	zip,	flip,
"f"	shelf,	cuff,	rough,	if,	puff.
"v"	verve,	live,	shave,	have,	shelve.
"ch"	lunch,	Mitch,	peach,	punch,	each.
"dg"	badge,	edge,	budge,	hedge,	Madge.

The consonants in the two groups of words on the following page use the *tongue* for articulation.

Example:

INITIAL CONSONANTS

"d"	dig,	dumb	dad —	dy,	doe.
"t"	Tim,	took,	toy,	tap,	tip.
"l"	love,	lift,	Lee,	lap,	loft.
"r"	ring,	rat,	red,	rope,	read.
"s"	sun,	sew,	soon,	sat,	sod.
"z"	zip,	zoo,	zone,	zap,	zoom.
"n"	need,	no,	noon,	nay,	knee.
"g"	go,	get,	give,	game,	gal.
"k"	keep,	kiss,	cool,	can,	Kim.

FINAL CONSONANTS

"d"	deed,	and,	sod,	head,	kid.
"t"	cat,	wept,	camped,	loft,	tight.
"l"	bill,	yell,	call,	bell,	eel.
"r"	beer,	are,	mar,	chair,	jeer.
"s"	eats,	bus,	kiss,	pass,	pats.
"z"	buzz,	these,	pause,	paws,	doze.
"n"	moon,	then,	won,	ton,	din.
"g"	gag,	frog,	mug,	egg,	big.
"k"	kick,	Mike,	bank,	cake,	ache.
"ng"	bang,	sing,	song,	long,	wrong.

There are three nasal consonants in English in which the sound is emitted through the nose ("m," "n," "ng"). These are voiced consonants which have pitch and can be prolonged to gain emotional effect, particularly at the end of words. These three nasal consonants are the only speech sounds in English that are produced with a lowered soft palate, thus allowing air to enter the nasal passages.

Use a 1 − 2 − 3 − 2 − 1 pattern in the next two groups of words. Be sure to sing the consonant on the same pitch as the vowel it precedes or follows. Don't scoop up to the pitch.

NOTE: In addition to learning how to articulate consonants clearly, singers must also learn to sing them in such a way that they do not detract from a legato melody line.

Example:

INITIAL NASAL CONSONANTS

"m" mean,___ mill,___ met,___ mop,___ moon.
"n" neat,___ knee,___ nod,___ note,___ nay.

FINAL NASAL CONSONANTS

"m" them,___ home,___ team,___ came,___ doom.
"n" noon,___ can,___ tin,___ ten,___ ban.
"ng" hang,___ wing,___ dong,___ hung,___ ring.

Although some consonants are voiced (such as the ones above), there are others that do not use vocal-cord vibration during production. They are called "voiceless" or "whispered" consonants.

Example:

INITIAL VOICELESS CONSONANTS

sun,___ fin,___ share,___ thin,___ help.
pat,___ took,___ keep,___ chew,___ soon.

FINAL VOICELESS CONSONANTS

eats, ___   cuff, ___   ash, ___   bath, ___   kick.
cup, ___   pint, ___   nook, ___   pinch, ___   sis.

In addition to exercises such as those presented in this chapter, student singers practice many other exercises (under the direction of their teacher) to promote greater skills in vocal flexibility, agility, power, strength, and endurance. Understanding the vocal instrument and refining its innate abilities enable voice students to sing with appropriate knowledge, expression, beauty, creativity, and joy. We hope that in ANYONE CAN SING you have found a measure of each.

A FINAL WORD

Now that you have read the informational material about singing and have practiced the exercises faithfully, it may be interesting and valuable for you to re-evaluate how you feel about your potential for learning to sing more successfully in the future. Therefore, we conclude with one of the evaluation charts introduced at the beginning OF ANYONE CAN SING.

We hope that with the help of this book you have made some progress toward the vocal goals identified in your Voice Evaluation Chart on page xvi. We also hope that you will continue singing and learning to sing better. Anyone can sing . . . especially you!

JOAN AND RICKY

MY POTENTIAL FOR FUTURE SUCCESS IN SINGING

How do you rate the POSSIBILITY of your achieving singing success in the future (i.e., singing songs beautifully and effectively)? This is not being asked to determine whether you actually want to perform or to seek a professional career. But, IF you DID want to, what do you think your chances would be for success?

I could do anything with my voice.
I could be as good as the most accomplished
professional singer.   _____   100% Perfect

I could sing well enough to be a   _____   90%
successful professional singer.

I could sing successfully in semi-   _____   80%
professional local productions.

                                                  _____   70%

I could sing solos effectively in amateur
groups. I could be a strong choir member.

                                                  _____   60%

I could participate comfortably and
securely in group singing.   _____   50% Average

I could learn to sing well enough for my   _____   40%
own pleasure and enjoy it.

                                                  _____   30%

I could learn to sing better, but still not
very well; not always on pitch; couldn't   _____   20%
learn to carry a tune flawlessly.

                                                  _____   10%

I couldn't sing at all. I couldn't learn.
There's no hope for improvement.   _____   0%   Totally
                                                                 Inadequate